THE
ULTIMATE
Rose
BOOK

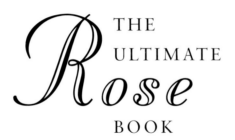

THE ULTIMATE

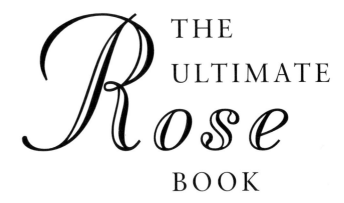

Rose

BOOK

PETER McHOY

HERMES HOUSE

This edition published in 2001 by Hermes House

Hermes House is an imprint of
Anness Publishing Limited
Hermes House
88–89 Blackfriars Road
London SE1 8HA

A CIP catalogue record for this book is available from the British Library.

Publisher: Joanna Lorenz
Editorial Manager: Helen Sudell
Designer: Bet Ayer
Additional text by: Gilly Love
Production Controller: Don Campaniello

The publishers would like to thank the following people for designing the projects in this book:
Fiona Barnett, Penny Boylan, Louise Brownlow, Andi Clevely, Stephanie Donaldson, Kally Ellis, Tessa Evelegh, Lucinda Ganderton,
Christine Kingdom, Gilly Love, Terence Moore, Ercole Moroni, Emma Petitt, Katherine Richmond, Isabel Stanley, Liz Trigg, Sally
Walton, Stewart Walton and Pamela Westland. The publishers would like to credit the following photographers:
James Duncan, John Freeman, Michelle Garrett, Nelson Hargreaves, Debbie Patterson, Graham Rae and Peter Williams.

Printed and bound in China

5 7 9 10 8 6

Contents

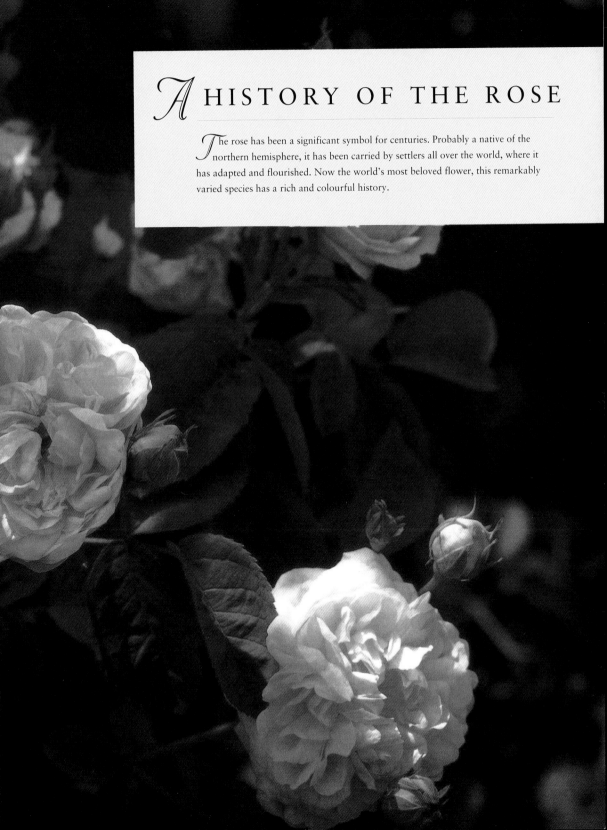

A HISTORY OF THE ROSE

The rose has been a significant symbol for centuries. Probably a native of the northern hemisphere, it has been carried by settlers all over the world, where it has adapted and flourished. Now the world's most beloved flower, this remarkably varied species has a rich and colourful history.

A HISTORY OF THE ROSE

Prized, cherished and fought over for centuries, roses now grow all over the world, although they are almost certainly indigenous to the northern hemisphere. Rose fossils, millions of years old, have been found only north of the equator, suggesting that those species now growing in South Africa, South America, Australia and New Zealand were taken there by emigrants.

ANCIENT ROSES

The wild rose was most certainly enjoyed by early people for its sweet petals and tasty hips, and rose cultivation probably began around 5,000 years ago in China and in what is now Iraq. In the *Iliad*, Homer's epic composed around 1200 BC, the poet tells of Achilles' shield being decorated with roses to celebrate his victory over Hector. Hector's body was anointed with rose oil before it was embalmed.

The roses mentioned by many Greek historians were almost certainly *Rosa gallica*, the ancestor of numerous European roses. Known as the 'Apothecary's Rose' or 'Red Damask', *R. g. officinalis* was the main source of rose oil and medicinal remedies in Europe until the introduction of rose species from the Far East.

The early Christian church condemned roses as a symbol of depravity, with some justification since Nero's obsession with these

PREVIOUS PAGE: 'Rosa 'Duchesse de Montebello'.

flowers almost certainly contributed to the fall of the Roman Empire. The emperor's excesses were notorious and it is said that tons of roses were required for the numerous banquets he gave where guests sat on pillows stuffed with them. Vast quantities of petals were showered over people at orgies, reputedly suffocating at least one participant, and pure rose-water baths were offered to all the guests.

Roses symbolized success in Roman times and millions of petals were threaded on to brass wires to make garlands and headdresses. Peasants consequently came to believe that it was more profitable to grow roses than corn, a disastrous misconception noted by the Roman poet Horace and other intellectuals of his time.

ABOVE: A descendant of the ancient gallica roses 'Cardinal de Richelieu' is a sumptuous purple rose raised in France in 1840.

BELOW: One of the best-known and most ancient of all historic roses, R. gallica officinalis, the 'Apothecary's Rose' or 'Red Damask', was widely grown for its scent in the Middle Ages.

ABOVE: *Adopted by the House of York as their emblem during the Wars of the Roses in fifteenth-century England,* Rosa x alba *is still sometimes grown in gardens. This is 'Semiplena', a semi-double variety still grown in some parts of the world for the production of attar.*

THE MIDDLE AGES

Little information exists about the cultivation of roses following the collapse of the Roman Empire until about AD 400, when the church adopted the white *R. alba* as the emblem of the Virgin Mary.

In 1272 Edward I of England, upon his return from the last Crusade, ordered rose trees to be planted in the gardens of the Tower of London and chose a gold rose as his own symbol.

It is possible that returning Crusaders were responsible for the introduction of *R. damascena*. Certainly by the end of the fifteenth century the rose 'Autumn Damask', known in France as 'Quatre Saisons'

and the first rose in Europe to produce two crops of flowers every summer, was growing in English gardens.

It is debatable whether *R. gallica* was brought to England by the Romans or at a later date by returning Crusaders. It was, however, the emblem of the House of Lancaster in the prolonged struggle against the house of York (who adopted *R. x alba*) during the bitter Wars of the Roses in England in the fifteenth century.

The marriage of Henry Tudor (Henry VII) and Elizabeth of York finally united the factions. Their emblem was a white rose in the centre of a red rose entwined with a crown. Since then the British royal family have adopted the rose as their own.

By the end of the sixteenth century, *R. foetida* had been introduced into Europe from what was then Persia and *R. moschata*, the musk rose, was certainly favoured by the court of Henry VIII.

ABOVE: *Rosa gallica versicolor or 'Rosa Mundi' is a striped sport from* R. g. officinalis *first recorded in 1581.*

European roses were taken to America by the Pilgrim Fathers and by the beginning of the seventeenth century were growing in many gardens in Massachusetts. North America already had its own species, R. *virginiana* and R. *carolina*. Another, R. *setigera*, would later produce some vigorous rambler cultivars including the pale pink 'Baltimore Belle', still famous in America, and the climber 'Long John Silver', a fragrant pure white.

EARLY HYBRIDS

Until the process of hybridization was understood in the nineteenth century, new rose varieties were the results of natural crosses or sports (mutations), carefully chosen and nurtured by gardeners and nurserymen. Dutch breeders pioneered work in Europe in the seventeenth century, working on R. *centifolia*, or the Provence Rose,

ABOVE: 'Old Blush', now more correctly called R. x odorata 'Pallida', is one of the original China roses. Its scent and long flowering season ensure that it is still planted by rose lovers.

ABOVE: 'Little White Pet' (1879) is a dwarf shrub which originated in the USA as a sport of the vigorous rambler 'Félicité et Perpétue'.

also known as the cabbage rose because of its "hundred-leaved" flowers. Moss roses appeared around the mid-eighteenth century as a sport (mutation) from R. *centifolia*.

Rose breeding was given tremendous impetus by the patronage of the Empress Josephine, wife of Napoleon. Between 1803 and 1814 she commissioned botanists and nurserymen all over the world to discover and breed new roses for her garden at Malmaison near Paris, where she eventually grew over 250 varieties.

INTRODUCTIONS FROM THE FAR EAST

The Chinese had been growing roses for thousands of years, and these began to reach European growers in the late eighteenth century. Around 1781 a pink rose, R. *chinensis*, now known as 'Old Blush', was planted in the Netherlands and soon came to

England. Some years later a captain of the British East India Company returned home with a red form of the same rose, which he had found growing in Calcutta, and it was named R. *semperflorens*, the 'Bengal Rose', or 'Slater's Crimson China'. Between them, these two roses are responsible for the remontant or repeat-flowering qualities in most modern roses.

At the beginning of the nineteenth century the flowers known as tea roses arrived on the ships of the British East India Company – their main cargo was tea, which probably accounts for the common name of these roses. They became fashionable in Europe, but because many of them are tender the Victorians grew them in grand conservatories, along with other exotic flowers brought back by explorers and botanists from all parts of the British empire.

ABOVE: 'Souvenir de la Malmaison', a famous old Bourbon rose, has beautiful quartered flowers in soft powder pink. There is a climbing as well as a bush form.

ABOVE: 'Madame Alfred Carrière', a Noisette climber raised in 1879, is still widely grown in gardens and is especially valued because it will grow successfully on a north-facing wall.

EAST MEETS WEST

One of the first marriages between a rose from the West and one from the East was a cross between 'Autumn Damask' and a red China rose which was probably obtained from France by the second Duchess of Portland, an enthusiastic rose collector of the late eighteenth century. The Portland roses, as they became known, were very popular in the early 1800s. Though few survive today, they are ideal for growing in containers and are prized for their perfume and ability to flower throughout the summer.

Meanwhile, at around the same time in Charleston, South Carolina, a rice-grower called John Champneys crossed a musk rose, *R. moschata*, with a China rose, *R. chinensis* 'Parson's Pink China' or 'Old Blush', which had been a gift from his friend and neighbour, Philippe Noisette. He

gave the new seedling to Noisette, who made more crosses and sent both seed and plants to his brother Louis in Paris. The first seedlings he called 'Rosier de Philippe Noisette', a long name that inevitably came to be shortened to 'Noisette'.

'Blush Noisette' is still widely grown today and so too is the beautiful 'Madame Alfred Carrière', one of the few climbing roses that can tolerate a north-facing wall.

Bourbon roses also made their appearance during this period. These began as a cross between 'Old Blush' and 'Autumn Damask' found growing in rose hedges on the Ile de Bourbon in the Indian Ocean. Many of these shrub roses are still available, including 'Louise Odier', 'Souvenir de la Malmaison' and the much-prized, thornless 'Zéphirine Drouhin'.

ABOVE: The beautiful Bourbon climber 'Zéphirine Drouhin' dates from 1868 and is greatly valued for its virtually thornless stems and long flowering season.

THE MODERN ROSE

Throughout the nineteenth century hybrid perpetuals were introduced as a result of breeding between Chinas, Portlands, Bourbons and Noisettes.

The birth of what is considered to be the first modern rose, the large-flowered or hybrid tea rose, took place in 1867 with the introduction of Jean-Baptiste Guillot's 'La France'. This new breed of roses satisfied gardeners' demands for neat, repeat-flowering and truly hardy shrubs with elegant and delicate flowers.

In the mid-eighteenth century a wild rambler, *R. multiflora*, had been introduced from Japan. In the hands of nineteenth-century breeders, it was to become the parent of the numerous cluster-flowered or floribunda roses of today.

Most rose-breeders of the twentieth century have concentrated their efforts on floribunda and hybrid tea roses, in colours echoing current tastes in fashion. Since the late 1960s there has been a steady increase in the number of smaller shrubs for tiny gardens, patios and pots.

At the same time, a new breed of roses, evocative of Dutch old masters and the romantic paintings of Pierre-Joseph Redouté, has been introduced by the English rose-grower David Austin. He has raised roses that may be described as some of the finest reproductions, growing no more than 1.2 m (4 ft) tall but with all the charm and scent of classic roses of the past, crossing damasks and gallicas with modern shrub roses. Now owners of even the smallest garden may enjoy the delights of roses that the Empress Josephine would have considered for her garden at Malmaison.

ABOVE: 'Graham Thomas' is one of the most popular of the modern shrub roses bred by David Austin in his series of "English" roses. It combines the form and fragrance of an old rose with a pure yellow colouring that nineteenth-century breeders could not achieve.

ABOVE: 'L. D. Braithwaite' is an outstanding modern shrub rose, with all the charm of the old-fashioned roses.

CLASSIFICATION OF ROSES

The long and eventful history of rose breeding means that today's rose lovers can enjoy an enormous variety of beautiful plants. We have come to expect a great deal from roses, and with thoughtful choice and careful cultivation they reward us with glorious flowers from spring until the dark days of winter; scent that fills the summer garden and lingers on in oils, preserves and pot-pourri; and decorative hips,

leaves and even thorns. There are forms and styles suitable for nearly every situation, from diminutive patio bushes to huge ramblers cascading in luxurious swags from trees and arbours.

There are several thousand documented roses, including original species and scores of hybrids that have been cultivated during the last four centuries. New rose hybrids are being introduced every year in

addition to older hybrids being rediscovered all over the world.

In 1971, the World Federation of Rose Societies reclassified both ancient and modern roses into more clearly defined garden groups. Broadly speaking, the era of the modern rose began in 1867 with the introduction of the first hybrid tea 'La France'. The various wild species form another group, divided into climbing and non-climbing species.

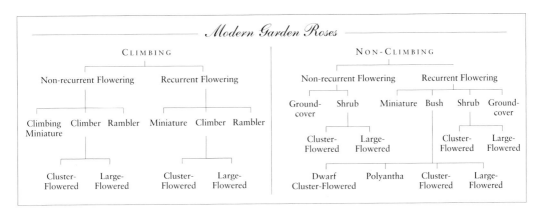

Modern Garden Roses

CLIMBING

Non-recurrent Flowering — Recurrent Flowering

Climbing Miniature · Climber · Rambler | Miniature · Climber · Rambler

Cluster-Flowered · Large-Flowered | Cluster-Flowered · Large-Flowered

NON-CLIMBING

Non-recurrent Flowering — Recurrent Flowering

Ground-cover · Shrub | Miniature · Bush · Shrub · Ground-cover

Cluster-Flowered · Large-Flowered | Cluster-Flowered · Large-Flowered

Dwarf Cluster-Flowered · Polyantha · Cluster-Flowered · Large-Flowered

What's in a Name?

Although it is more than 25 years since the new classifications were recommended, both gardeners and growers tend to cling to the old names with which most are familiar. Cluster-flowered roses are still likely to be described as floribundas, and large-flowered roses referred to as hybrid teas, in many catalogues, on labels in rose gardens, and in everyday conversation. For reasons of familiarity the terms "floribunda"

and "hybrid tea" have been used freely in this book.

In addition to the "official" categories, catalogues sometimes describe varieties as "patio roses". These are low-growing floribundas suitable for patio beds and even containers. Some of the smallest patio roses are similar in size to the largest of the miniatures.

Catalogues sometimes use a grower's code name for the variety as well

as the name under which it is widely known and distributed. For example, 'Sexy Rexy' is the selling name of 'Macrexy' (bred by McGredy), and 'Paul Shirville' is the selling name of 'Harqueterwife' (bred by Harkness). The breeder's name is a way of identifying a variety if the local name is changed when the rose is sold in different countries. It is also the name likely to be used during early trials, before the variety is released to the public.

GROWING BETTER ROSES

*T*his practical section covers how to choose the right rose for your garden and includes step-by-step instructions on how to plant, prune and tend your roses. It also provides a useful year-round breakdown of essential rose care.

Growing Better Roses

Roses respond well to a little tender, loving care. If you feed them well and make sure they do not become stressed through lack of water or by pests or diseases, they will reward you for many years with superb displays of beautiful flowers and lush, healthy foliage.

Pruning will also ensure vigorous plants with plenty of blooms. For the best results, however, you do need to know how best to prune each kind of rose and step-by-step instructions on pages 26–37 show how easy and uncomplicated it can be.

Roses are remarkably tough and adaptable, and will go on growing with minimal attention for many years, but they will deteriorate and flower less prolifically, with smaller blooms, on bushes that become poorly shaped. Simple routine care makes an enormous difference, and the benefits will be obvious: lush, compact growth, an abundance of flowers, and blooms and foliage unmarred by pests such as aphids or diseases like mildew.

The regular but simple tasks required during the spring and summer are no hardship to a rose enthusiast. Close regular contact with the plants means that problems are quickly spotted and will seldom become serious. From spring pruning until the first bloom of the season, there is the thrill of anticipation.

PREVIOUS PAGE: Rosa 'Heidi'.

ABOVE: During the dormant season, bare-root plants are often sold with a wrap to protect their roots. If it is too frosty or wet to plant them, healthy roses can be left in the wrappings for a short time until conditions improve.

ABOVE: If you are buying in a shop or garden centre, avoid roses with elongated, new pale shoots, which might indicate long and incorrect storage. This plant has been on sale in the shop for too long.

ABOVE: Container-grown roses should have plenty of fine roots around the edge of the root-ball, but not lots of them winding their way around the edge of the pot.

Frequent close observation shows all the promise of new shoots and then buds growing by the week, with a freshness of foliage which is not matched later in the year.

Working among roses in flower, whether dead-heading or even weeding, is a fragrant and delightful task that brings intimate contact with these most wonderful flowers.

LEFT: Rosa odorata 'Mutabilis' is a China rose of unknown origin, which displays beautifully subtle changes of colour as it ages.

Buying Roses

Roses are sold either container-grown or as bare-root plants (these have been lifted from the field while dormant and the soil shaken off). Bare-root plants sold in shops and garden centres usually have their roots packed in moss or peat, and wrapped in moisture-retaining plastic.

Container-grown plants are available all year round, and can be planted any time the ground is not frozen or waterlogged. Bare-root plants are available only in the dormant season, usually between mid- or late autumn and early spring.

Plants ordered by post from specialist rose nurseries will probably arrive bare-root – testimony to the fact that these plants establish themselves readily if moved when dormant. The quality of bare-root plants from a specialist nursery is usually high and the plants arrive in good condition as they are freshly lifted and have not spent weeks in a shop or garden centre.

RIGHT: When choosing a container-grown rose, look for a plant with a well-balanced basic structure of healthy stems, whether you are buying a ground cover rose (left), when you should see low, horizontal shoots, or a climber (right) with strong upright growth.

PLANTING

A rose is a long-term investment, and will give decades of pleasure if it is looked after. Get it off to a good start with thorough soil preparation and careful planting.

PREPARING THE SOIL

It is a myth that roses only grow well on heavy clay soils: many excellent rose gardens are on light and sandy soils. There is, however, some truth behind the popular belief. Many modern roses tolerate such a wide range of soils only because they are budded on to appropriate rootstocks; plants growing in light and "hungry"

soils require more feeding, watering and mulching.

Albas, gallicas, damasks, centifolias, Portlands and moss roses can cope with less fertile soils than modern hybrids, as can species roses such as *R. rugosa* and *R. pimpinellifolia*.

The ideal soil has a pH of around 6.5–7 (slightly acid to neutral). A simple and inexpensive soil test kit will give the pH and instructions for how to modify it if necessary.

Dig over the site to loosen the soil and remove weeds, mixing in as much organic material as possible. Garden compost or well-rotted manure are

ideal. If the supply is limited, incorporate it around the root area when planting rather than spreading it thinly while digging. If you find a hard, compacted layer when soil to the depth of a spade's blade has been removed, ensure the ground below is broken up with a fork to improve drainage.

If other roses have previously been growing in the same spot in recent years, remove as much of the old soil as possible and replace it with fresh (or plant your new rose in a different position) to reduce the risk of replant disease.

PLANTING A BARE-ROOT ROSE

1 Dig a hole large enough to take the roots when spread out, and deep enough not to bend them. Incorporate garden compost or well-rotted manure in the base if not already added to the soil when preparing the bed.

2 Work a handful of bonemeal into the planting hole (wear gloves), then spread the roots out evenly, with the plant placed centrally. If the roots grow in just one direction, do not bend them, but plant the rose to one side of the hole.

3 Trickle the soil between the roots, shaking the plant occasionally as the hole is filled to settle the soil. Tread around the base of the plant to firm the soil, and make sure the budding union is completely covered to prevent suckers.

1 Excavate a hole approximately twice the width of the container, and a little deeper. Break up the soil in the bottom with a fork, incorporating humus-forming material such as garden compost or well-rotted manure, if this has not already been done during general preparation of the bed.

2 Remove the rose from its pot, gently tease out some of the roots from around the edge to encourage them to grow out into the surrounding soil, then position the root-ball in the hole. Lay a cane across the hole to check the depth, adding or removing soil as necessary.

3 The graft union (the point where the rose was budded on to its rootstock) should be about 2.5 cm (1 in) below the level of the surrounding bed. Backfill with soil and firm in with your foot to ensure there are no large air pockets where the roots could dry out.

4 If planting in spring or early summer, apply a rose or general garden fertilizer and fork it in lightly. Water well, then mulch with more organic material, such as garden compost or chipped bark, to reduce water evaporation and help suppress weeds.

ROUTINE ROSECARE

Roses respond to care and attention, but especially to feeding, watering and mulching. Simple tasks like dead-heading and removing suckers also improve the appearance of the rose garden as well as ensuring that the plants remain in tip-top condition and bloom prolifically.

FEEDING

Roses are "hungry" shrubs and require feeding if they are to grow to their maximum potential. If any of the important nutrients are deficient, the plant will show symptoms such as weak or stunted growth, small or discoloured leaves and small, poor quality flowers.

Feeding starts at planting time. Plenty of humus-forming material such as garden compost or well-rotted manure adds nutrients as well as improving soil structure. The initial nutrients are soon depleted, but a soil with a high organic content is more likely to retain nutrients that you apply later than, for instance, a light, sandy soil from which fertilizers are quickly leached.

Organic mulches applied annually also help to top up the humus in the soil as they rot down.

It is possible to grow good roses simply by applying plenty of manure or garden compost each year, but for optimum performance an additional boost is required.

Enthusiasts use rose fertilizers that are specially formulated, but where

ABOVE: *Scatter granular or powdered fertilizer in a circle around the base of the plant, but keep it away from the stem.*

ABOVE: *Hoe the fertilizer in so that it penetrates more readily. If it is dry, water in thoroughly.*

just a few roses are grown it may be cheaper or more convenient to use the same general balanced garden fertilizer bought for other flowering plants. Apply the first dose in spring before the leaves open fully, and another one in early or mid-summer when the roses are blooming freely. Follow the instructions on the packet for application rates.

Avoid feeding in late summer as this may encourage the plant to produce soft growth that could be damaged in a cold winter.

Liquid feeding will give roses a useful quick-acting boost, so if other garden plants are being fed from a hose-end dilutor, for example, give the roses a dose if they do not appear to be in tip-top condition.

WATERING

Roses have deep roots, so they do not show signs of water stress until a drought is prolonged, but their growth will probably be impaired, and the flowers smaller.

If water has to be rationed, always give priority to roses planted within the last year. More established bushes are better able to cope with dry soil. Never allow newly planted roses to become dry at the roots.

Try to water thoroughly if there are no restrictions. At any time, one thorough soaking is better than regular dribbles. As a guide, apply 4–5 litres (1 gallon) for a rose bush, three times this for a climber. Water in the evening, when less moisture will be lost through evaporation.

For a large rose bed or border, a permanently installed trickle irrigation hose that can be turned on when required is ideal.

MULCHING

A mulch serves three main purposes: it suppresses weeds, reduces moisture loss through evaporation, and in some cases improves the appearance of the bed.

Plastic mulching sheets are effective, but visually unattractive. They are best used for newly planted roses, and then covered with a thin layer of a more decorative mulch such as chipped bark.

Organic mulches should be applied at least 5 cm (2 in) thick to suppress weeds, when used alone, but should be kept clear of the stems of the roses.

Chipped bark is a popular and efficient mulch, and it looks good. Cocoa shells can also be used, but they may blow about when dry. Rotted manure and garden compost make excellent mulches and add nutrients, but they are not decorative.

ABOVE: *Chipped bark is a widely available mulch and is visually more pleasing than bare soil.*

ABOVE: *Cocoa shells are sometimes used as a mulch. When fresh they are an attractive brown, but this gradually weathers to a more earthy colour.*

Grass clippings can be used as long as a hormone weedkiller has not been used on the grass, but they can look unattractive as they begin to rot.

Spring is the best time to apply a mulch, as the soil is warmed up. Ensure that the ground is moist before mulching.

Organic mulches require topping up occasionally. This is best done in spring or early summer.

LEFT: *Strawy manure will help to add plenty of humus to the soil as it slowly rots down, but it is not as attractive as chipped bark.*

BELOW: *Rotted manure makes an ideal mulch for roses, and it soon blends in with the soil.*

DEAD-HEADING

Most roses benefit from dead-heading, especially hybrid teas and floribundas, but do not remove the heads of roses grown for their decorative hips. Removing dead flowers as they fade helps to promote the production of fresh blooms on repeat-flowering roses and improves the appearance of those with a single flush – such as 'Albertine' – whose flowers do not shed their petals and become unsightly as they age.

Although individual flowers can be removed as they fade, this may be too time-consuming if there are many roses in the garden. But at least remove the whole truss when all the blooms have faded, cutting the stem back to the second or third leaf below the flower truss. If the plant is still young, however, do not cut back the stem so hard.

RIGHT: Dead-heading keeps the bushes looking tidy, and it ensures the plant puts most of its energy into producing new growth.

SUCKERS

While dead-heading, keep an eye open for suckers – shoots growing from the rootstock at the base of the plant (or higher up the stem in the case of a standard). Suckers can easily take over the plant and should be removed by pulling each one off at the point of origin. Snipping off the suckers may only encourage more of them to grow.

Suckers look different to the stems of the grafted rose. The leaves may be a different colour, or smaller than those of the variety, and may have seven leaflets instead of five.

1 Remove suckers at their point of origin, which usually involves pulling away some of the soil.

2 If possible, pull them off, otherwise try to cut them off flush with the main stem.

ROSE HEALTHCARE

Roses are popular with pests as well as people. Unfortunately they are prone to pests such as greenfly and diseases like blackspot and mildew, as well as a number of less serious problems. All of these can be controlled, but vigilance is required to nip problems in the bud.

Incidence of disease and pest attack is influenced to some extent by the climate and regional variations: blackspot is more prevalent in some areas than in others, mildew is more likely to be a problem if the weather is damp, and greenfly populations are partly governed by the winter survival of their predators.

Some rose varieties are more susceptible to problems than others, but well-fed roses that are growing strongly usually shake off the effects of any attack more readily, especially if quick action is taken. Avoid introducing pests or disease into your garden by alway buying good-quality roses.

The following are some of the problems likely to be encountered in the garden.

ABOVE: It is almost inevitable that aphids such as greenfly or blackfly will attack at some point during the season. The best control is vigilance and quick action with an appropriate insecticide.

APHIDS

How to identify: The aphid that most commonly attacks roses is greenfly, usually spotted near the start of the growing season on the tips of stems and on developing flower buds.
Control: Spray the plants with a proprietary systemic insecticide as soon as an infestation is noticed,

and repeat as directed by the manufacturer. Some insecticides are selective in their action and leave beneficial insects such as ladybirds unharmed.

Alternatively, spray with a solution of washing-up liquid or even with plain water, to disperse the pest, though such treatments will have to be repeated daily.

Though infestations are sometimes heavy, the pest is easy to control and long-term damage can be avoided.

BALLING

How to identify: Petals turn brown and cling together so that the flower fails to open. Most likely in wet weather.
Control: None possible. Balling is a seasonal problem that does not affect the overall health of the plant, but it is worth removing balled flowers. Apart from their unsightly appear-

ance, they are prone to rot, which may allow other diseases to take hold. Roses with very delicate petals are particularly susceptible.

BLACKSPOT

How to identify: Black spots or patches develop on the leaves and, in some cases, the stems, from mid-summer onwards. The leaves yellow and eventually drop off. Plants left untreated may eventually die back.
Control: Remove all infected leaves and stems and destroy them, then spray the plant with an appropriate fungicide. If you need to cut the plant hard back, feed and water well to encourage a quick recovery. Blackspot is more common in certain geographical areas and some rose varieties are more susceptible than others. Where blackspot is known to be a problem, spray with a fungicide as a precaution. In severe cases, replace the plants with disease-resistant varieties.

ABOVE: Balling is caused by wet weather. It is not a common problem but some varieties are prone to it.

mildew

rust

LEFT: *Symptoms of the three most serious rose diseases.*

blackspot

PROLIFERATION

How to identify: An unusual condition in which the stem continues to grow through the open flower, producing a further bud or cluster of buds. It is usually caused by damage to the stem while it is growing, perhaps by frost or a virus.

Control: Cut off affected stems. If only one or a few stems are affected, further steps are unnecessary, but where the whole plant has the condition a virus is probably the culprit and the whole plant should be dug up and destroyed.

ABOVE: *Proliferation is an unusual physiological disorder, perhaps caused by injury to the growing tip. In most cases, cutting out the affected stem is all that is necessary.*

MILDEW

How to identify: A whitish-grey powdering on the leaves and stems, which if not treated may cover the whole plant.

Control: Spray with a proprietary fungicide. Thin out congested growth. Where the overall planting is thick, and air circulation is therefore poor, replant to ensure more space around the plants.

RUST

How to identify: Orange spots that turn to black appear on the undersides of leaves from mid-summer onwards. If left untreated, rose rust can be fatal to the plant.

Control: Remove infected parts then spray with an appropriate fungicide (some fungicides are not very effective against rose rust). Thin out growth and improve air circulation around the plants as for mildew.

DIEBACK

How to identify: Flower buds, where present, fail to mature and wither. Beginning at the tip of the stem, leaves begin to wither and drop off. The stem itself droops and may blacken.

Control: Cut back all affected growth to healthy wood, then feed the plant well during the growing season to encourage new growth.

REPLANT DISEASE

How to identify: The roses suddenly fail to thrive and begin to die back. It usually occurs where roses have been grown in the same soil for many years.

Control: Dig up and discard the affected roses, then replace the top 30 cm (12 in) of the soil with fresh topsoil. Replant with fresh stock.

PRUNING: HYBRID TEAS

Hybrid tea (large-flowered) roses usually have large, fully double flowers with a high pointed centre, though as new varieties are developed the distinction between these and some floribundas (cluster-flowered roses) is becoming less clear than it used to be. A good rose catalogue will tell you whether your rose is a hybrid tea variety, but it is not serious if you get it wrong. Even if a hybrid tea is pruned as a floribunda there will still be a pleasing display of flowers.

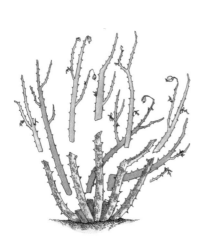

ABOVE: *To make the pruning easier, start by cutting out any badly positioned, diseased or dead wood (shown here coloured brown) close to the base. This will leave fewer stems about which pruning decisions have to be made, and the extra space makes the job easier. Shorten the remaining stems by about half, cutting to an outward-facing bud whenever possible.*

1 Hybrid tea roses look very different depending on whether or not they have been pruned regularly. This rose has been pruned annually and is not particularly congested. If you have a rose that has not been pruned for many years, there will be more dead wood and crossing shoots to be removed, but otherwise pruning is exactly the same. Start by cutting out dead or diseased shoots. This will make it easier to see what remains to be done.

3 (Right) Prune all the main stems by about half, or to within 20–25 cm (8–10 in) of the ground. The exact amount you cut off is not critical and is a matter of personal experience and choice. Try to bear in mind the final shape of the bush. Wherever possible, prune to an outward-pointing bud to give the bush more spread rather than a congested centre.

2 Remove badly placed, crossing or very congested shoots. Most of these can be cut back to their point of origin, but if growth is sparse cut to just above a healthy bud, close to the base. Prune out or shorten any very thin, spindly shoots. If there are plenty of other shoots, cut back to the point of origin. If there are few shoots, you may prefer to cut back to about two or three buds from the base of the shoot.

4 *(Above)* This is what the bush will probably look like after pruning. Although it is sparse at this stage, vigorous new growth will soon transform its appearance.

5 *(Right)* This is what can be expected a few months later if a hybrid tea rose has been pruned properly: even healthy growth and plenty of perfect flowers.

You Can Be Rough!

If you have a lot of roses to prune, simply going over the rose bed with a powered hedge-trimmer (shears) may be an appealing option. To traditionalists this sounds horrifying, but trials of the "rough and ready" method have shown that floribundas and hybrid teas can actually produce a better display than when pruned conventionally. However, there could be drawbacks: the bushes may become too congested, diseases may become a problem due to the more congested growth and because the dead wood on each plant is not being monitored individually.

For a general garden display, however, this method is well worth considering, especially if you keep an eye open for dead or diseased shoots to prune out at the same time.

Although a powered hedge-trimmer will save time, you can use secateurs for the same kind of effect, just topping the shoots at the required level.

RIGHT: As part of a trial these roses were pruned with a hedge-trimmer. Despite this crude treatment, they performed just as well the following summer as roses pruned in the traditional way.

PRUNING: FLORIBUNDAS

Floribunda roses, sometimes called cluster-flowered roses, have many flowers open at once in the same cluster, and are noted for their prolific blooming. Although most varieties have flattish flowers with relatively few petals, some have almost hybrid tea-shaped blooms with lots of petals and more pointed flowers. If in doubt, a good rose catalogue will tell you whether a particular variety is a floribunda – though no great harm will befall your rose if you get it wrong.

1 Floribunda roses often look more "twiggy" than hybrid teas, regardless of how they were pruned the previous year. Do not be deterred if they appear to have a confusing tangle of thorny shoots. After removing unhealthy shoots just start pruning from one side and work across each plant.

2 Start by cutting out dead or diseased shoots (ignore dieback at the tips of shoots at this stage, as they will probably be removed with the rest of the stem later). Cut these unwanted shoots back to their point of origin if there are plenty of other stems, otherwise to a point just above a healthy bud close to the base.

ABOVE: *First cut out any badly placed or very old shoots that are dying or diseased (shown coloured brown), then shorten the remaining main shoots to about 45 cm (18 in), or about half their length. Cut back to an outward-facing bud where possible.*

3 Next, remove any crossing or very badly placed branches. Cut out completely if necessary, or back to a bud pointing in a better direction. Also remove any very thin, spindly shoots coming from near the base of the bush.

4 Cut all the main stems back to about 45 cm (18 in), but use some discretion to reflect the size and vigour of the variety.

5 There will probably be some long sideshoots remaining on the main stems. Shorten these by cutting off between one-third and two-thirds of their length. Cut back to a bud pointing outwards rather than towards the centre of the bush.

6 This is what the bushes will probably look like after pruning. The framework is already well established, and new growth will soon restore the plants to their summer height.

7 A well-pruned floribunda rose will produce plenty of new, vigorous, even growth and an abundance of flowers.

Spread the Flowering

Although the bushes will look less even in growth, it is possible to extend the flowering season a little by leaving some shoots unpruned. These should flower earlier, followed by the pruned shoots. If this method is adopted, be sure to cut back the unpruned shoots the following year. Do not leave any shoots unpruned for more than two years.

When to Prune

For hybrid tea and floribunda roses, autumn and spring pruning both have their advocates. A good compromise is to shorten the height of very tall varieties by about half in the autumn, to reduce wind resistance that would cause wind-rock damage by loosening the roots. This is unnecessary with compact varieties. Most people prefer to prune their roses in early spring when new growth is beginning but before the leaves start to expand.

$\mathscr{P}$RUNING: SHRUB ROSES

$\mathscr{I}$n pruning terms, shrub roses include any species of wild rose and old-fashioned varieties of bushy roses that pre-date hybrid teas and floribundas. Modern shrub roses, raised in recent times but retaining many of the characteristics of the traditional old-fashioned types, are pruned in the same way.

They generally make much bigger bushes than hybrid tea and floribunda types, but do not require such regular or intensive pruning. The main objective of annual pruning is to prevent the bushes becoming too large or congested.

1 Most species and early shrub roses will continue to flower well even without pruning, but become large and congested. Pruning will improve the overall appearance and help to keep the shrub compact.

ABOVE: *Pruning should always be modified to suit the growth characteristics of the plant but, as a guide, shorten the main stems by between a quarter and a half, and any sideshoots that remain by about two-thirds. Cut out any badly positioned or diseased stems completely.*

2 After some years there will be a lot of very old wood, and probably congested stems. On an old plant, cut out one or two of the oldest or most congested shoots, taking them back to the base. Cut out any dead or diseased wood at the same time.

The rose illustrated naturally produces a lot of cane-like stems from the base; others will have fewer but thicker stems, more like those on a hybrid tea.

3 Shorten the main shoots (those that arise from the base of the plant, not sideshoots) by between a quarter and a half. If the shoot is 1.2 m (4 ft) tall, cut off 30–60 cm (1–2 ft).

If the shrub has also produced a lot of sideshoots (those growing off the main stems), shorten these by about two-thirds. If the sideshoot is 30 cm (12 in) long, cut back to about 10 cm (4 in).

4 Even when pruning has been done, you may be left with a substantial framework of stems. This is normal, as a shrub rose usually makes a large bush. With those that shoot freely from the base, like this one, you can be more drastic.

5 *(Left)* Annual pruning will ensure there is plenty of vigorous young growth from the base of the plant, keeping the size compact and ensuring plenty of flowers even close to the ground.

PRUNING: CLIMBERS

Climbing roses can seem daunting to prune. Not only is there physically a lot of growth to deal with, there are also different techniques to use according to the flowering habit of the variety. First decide whether the variety to be pruned is a repeat-flowerer, then follow the appropriate technique described.

ONCE-FLOWERING CLIMBERS

These have a permanent framework of woody stems, usually with very few new shoots growing from the base. They are best pruned in summer, when flowering has finished.

ABOVE: On a well-established once-flowering climber, cut out one or two of the oldest stems to a point just above a new shoot close to the base. If there are no suitable low-growing new shoots, choose a point higher up the plant where there is one. Dead-head all the remaining shoots.

1 Because these climbers have a stable framework of woody shoots, and are pruned in full leaf after flowering, they can often be intimidating to prune. Fortunately they usually flower well with minimal pruning, provided the plant is kept free of dead and diseased wood.

ABOVE: A climbing rose in full bloom.

2 Try to cut out one or two of the oldest stems (this will not be necessary on plants only a few years old), to increase the amount of new growth. If you can find a young replacement shoot near the base, cut to just above this. If there are no low-growing new shoots, choose a replacement perhaps 30–60 cm (1–2 ft) up the stem. Tie in the new growth to replace the shoot you have just removed.

Do not remove more than one-third of the stems, otherwise flowering will suffer the next year.

3 Go along the remaining stems and shorten the sideshoots to leave two or three buds.

REPEAT-FLOWERING CLIMBERS

These generally bloom from mid-summer through to autumn, although after the first flush the flowers may be fewer and more sporadic. The terms "perpetual-flowering" or "remontant" may also be used to describe these roses. They flower on new wood, but as relatively few new main shoots are produced, little pruning is required.

BELOW: A climbing rose trained up a tripod lends height to a border. Trim back any shoots that are growing too tall for the support.

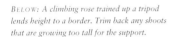

1 During the summer, dead-head as the flowers fade, unless the plant is too large for this to be practical. Cut back to the nearest leaf.

2 In early spring, just shorten the shoots that flowered the previous summer, if the plant is growing too tall. Drastic pruning or reshaping should not be necessary unless the rose has been neglected. After shortening the tips of the main shoots, go along each stem in turn to identify which sideshoots flowered in the summer and cut them back to two or three buds.

3 Remove entirely any shoots that are badly positioned, and cut out any dead or diseased wood. The basic outline of the rose may not look very different after pruning, but it will ensure that there are plenty of flowers in future years.

PRUNING: RAMBLERS

Rambler roses produce new stems freely from the base, rather than growing steadily taller on old stems. This gives them a lower, more spreading growth habit. They flower once – in mid- or late summer – and usually have large trusses of small blooms. As they flower on shoots produced the previous year, pruning is best done when flowering is over.

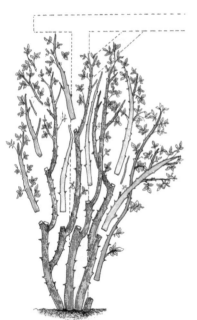

ABOVE: *Ramblers are straightforward to prune. Cut back old canes that have flowered, taking them back to a point where there is a new replacement shoot. Do not prune out an old shoot unless there is a new one to replace it, but remove completely any very old, dead or diseased wood.*

1 Prune after flowering – late summer is a good time. Old, congested plants can be more daunting than young ones, but they will not present a problem if the pruning is done methodically.

2 First cut out any dead or damaged shoots, or those that are very weak and spindly. Do not remove vigorous young shoots.

3 Cut out old spent canes that have flowered, but only where there are new shoots to replace them. Once you have a well-established rambler, try to balance the shoots that you remove with those available to replace them. This will vary from plant to plant and year to year. On any old flowered canes that have been retained, shorten the sideshoots to leave two or three leaves.

4 Tie in new shoots to the support. Wherever possible, tie loosely to horizontal wires or a trellis.

5 *(Opposite)* Rambler roses like this will flower prolifically every summer. Regular pruning ensures that old wood is replaced by vigorous new growth so that the plant is clothed with flowers from top to bottom.

Pillar Roses

Pillar roses are similar to ramblers but are grown in a column shape up a post or pillar. Growth is usually upright and the rather rigid stems are seldom much more than 2.4 m (8 ft) tall. They are repeat-flowering and bloom on the current season's wood. Good rose catalogues indicate which varieties are most suitable for growing in this way.

Pillar roses require regular pruning only once they are well established. Apart from cutting out one or two of the oldest stems each year, the only pruning required is to shorten shoots that have flowered to maintain an attractive shape. This is best done in late summer to early winter.

℘RUNING: STANDARDS

The pruning of standard roses can appear confusing, and even gardeners very confident about pruning bush roses sometimes feel uneasy about this task. However, if the pruning is directed to forming an attractive, rounded head, there are few difficulties.

Weeping standards are dealt with differently. These are pruned in summer – after flowering – and not in spring like a normal standard.

PRUNING A NORMAL STANDARD

1 (Right) Do not be deterred by the apparent tangle of shoots, just keep a rounded head in mind as you work through the pruning methodically.

BELOW: If it is well pruned in the dormant season, a standard rose will produce a rounded head of even growth that makes a ball of beautiful blooms.

ABOVE: Prune an ordinary standard rose (left) by shortening the summer's growth by about half. Prune a weeping standard (right) by cutting back each long shoot to a point where there is a new one to replace it. If no suitable replacement shoots can be found, do not prune the main stems; instead, shorten the sideshoots on the flowered stems to two buds.

2 During late winter or early spring, shorten the main stems in the head to about six buds, more or less depending on the age of the plant.

Do not prune too hard, as this may stimulate over-vigorous shoots that could spoil the shape. Cut to an outward-facing bud, to encourage a good shape.

3 Old plants may have areas of dead or diseased wood. Cut affected shoots back to healthy buds.

4 Shorten sideshoots growing from the main stem to a couple of buds, to stop growth becoming too congested.

5 (Right) Aim to leave a rounded head of reasonably evenly spaced branches. Although the rose looks unattractive at this stage, try to visualize it with the new shoots growing from this framework.

Pruning a Weeping Standard

Weeping standards, which sometimes have their shoots trained over an umbrella-shaped frame, are really rambling roses grafted on to a single stem. For this reason they are pruned like ramblers in summer or early autumn, when flowering has finished, and not in the dormant season.

If pruning is not done annually growth can become congested and tangled.

While pruning, take the opportunity to check that the stake is sound, and that ties are not too tight.

It takes a few years to produce a weeping rose as well clothed with flowering shoots as this. Once a good head has been achieved, maintain it by cutting some of the oldest shoots back to a point where there is a young replacement.

PROPAGATION

Propagating roses is satisfying and fun, and even if they are not needed for your own garden they make ideal gifts for friends.

Commercially, roses are budded on to rootstocks, but this is an impractical technique for amateurs, for whom rootstocks can be difficult to obtain. Fortunately, perfectly satisfactory roses can be grown from cuttings.

The bushes of some kinds, such as hybrid teas, may be less vigorous than those budded on to a rootstock, but climbers, ramblers and most shrub roses do very well on their own roots, and because there is no rootstock you will not have to worry about suckers.

Semi-ripe cuttings are taken in mid- or late summer, hardwood cuttings in autumn or early winter. Most gardeners find taking hardwood cuttings easier because this method does not require any special equipment and aftercare is minimal.

HARDWOOD CUTTINGS

Prepare a trench about 23–30 cm (9–12 in) deep in the open ground and line it to one-third of its depth with sharp sand.

Cut well-ripened, pencil-thick stems from the rose, remove the soft tip of each and trim to a length of about 23 cm (9 in), making the basal cut just below a leaf joint. Remove

any leaves that remain on the stem. Dip the base of each cutting in a rooting hormone, then place it in the trench, leaving about 7.5 cm (3 in) above the surface. Firm the cuttings in and water well.

If hard frosts cause soil erosion, it may be necessary to refirm the cuttings during the winter. Keep them well watered in dry weather and remove any flower buds that form during the growing season.

The cuttings should be rooted by the autumn following planting. If they are sufficiently developed they can be transferred to their final position in the garden; otherwise allow them to grow on for another year.

SEMI-RIPE CUTTINGS

1 Select a sideshoot that is still green but beginning to turn woody at the base. Cut just above an outward-facing bud.

2 Trim the cutting at the base, just below a leaf joint.

3 Trim back the soft tip to leave a stem about 10 cm (4 in) long.

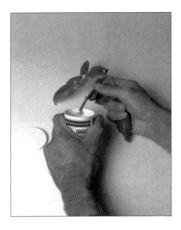  

4 Remove the lower leaves and any thorns. Dip the base of the cutting in a rooting hormone powder, and tap off the excess.

5 Fill a pot with a mixture of two parts sharp sand to one part peat. Use a small dibber to make holes, and insert the cuttings up to two-thirds of their length in the rooting medium.

6 Firm the cuttings into the soil with your fingers, then spray them gently with a copper fungicide to moisten the compost and kill off any fungal spores.

7 (*Left*) Label the cuttings, then enclose the pot in a clear plastic bag to prevent moisture loss. Support the bag with cane or wire hoops to prevent contact between the plastic and the leaves, as moisture from the condensation may cause the leaves to rot. Keep the cuttings in a shady, frost-free place until rooted.

ABOVE: *After about six to eight weeks, roots will start to form, as shown here, and the cuttings will begin to grow. The plants can slowly be hardened off, but do not be in too much of a hurry to pot them up individually. Wait until the roots are well formed.*

A YEAR IN THE ROSE GARDEN

Early spring

ABOVE: *Prune hybrid teas and floribundas once the winter frosts are over and as soon as new growth begins.*

• Improve the soil and plant new stock.
• Finish spring pruning before the new leaves emerge if possible.
• On all types of rose, cut out any dead, diseased or damaged wood.
• Hoe in a rose fertilizer around the bases of the plants as growth emerges, then water in well. If the ground has been mulched, draw back the mulch before applying the fertilizer.
• Mulch or top up an existing mulch.
• Renovate neglected plants by pruning and feeding.

Mid- and late spring

ABOVE: *Dig a generously sized hole in well-prepared soil when planting a container rose.*

• Check for signs of aphids such as greenfly, and begin pest control.
• Continue to plant new roses.

Early summer

ABOVE: *Rotted manure makes an effective mulch and also adds nutrients to the soil.*

• Control weeds.
• Mulch if you have not already done so, but choose a day when the ground is moist.
• Spray as necessary to control pests and diseases.

Mid-summer

ABOVE: *Try to find the time to remove individual spent flowers to keep roses looking their best.*

• Dead-head regularly except for varieties which have decorative hips.
• Feed with a rose fertilizer (or a general-purpose balanced fertilizer if you prefer).
• Increase your stock by taking semi-ripe cuttings.
• Check for, and control, blackspot, rust and mildew.
• Plant new container-grown stock.
• Trim rose hedges after flowering, unless they will have decorative hips.
• Prune ramblers and weeping standards when they have finished flowering.

LATE SUMMER

ABOVE: *Once you have pruned out old stems of ramblers and climbers, tie in vigorous new shoots to replace them.*

• Tie in strong new shoots of climbers and ramblers to extend the framework.
• Continue to take semi-ripe cuttings.
• Send off rose orders for autumn planting.

AUTUMN

• Hoe in bonemeal around the base of the plants, and water in well.
• Order new plants.
• Prepare and plant new beds.
• Take hardwood cuttings.
• In a windy or very exposed garden, shorten long shoots of hybrid tea and floribunda roses to reduce winter wind-rock (complete the pruning in spring).

RIGHT: *Choose a spare piece of ground that is airy but lightly shaded in which to plant hardwood cuttings.*

WINTER

• Tidy up hedges with ornamental hips (such as *Rosa rugosa*) that were not pruned after flowering.

• Plant new roses, provided the ground is not frozen or waterlogged.
• Prepare the ground for roses to be planted in spring.

ABOVE: *Dig a large hole when planting a bush, shrub, or old-fashioned rose. Add bonemeal to the soil that will surround the plant to promote root growth.*

ROSES AROUND THE GARDEN

Roses are a favourite with every gardening enthusiast. Even a solitary rose makes a great focal point in any part of the garden. The following section is a practical look at different planting methods and combinations that will inspire you to ever-greater creativity.

ROSES AROUND THE GARDEN

Roses are often grown in dedicated beds or in areas of the garden devoted solely to them, but they are very versatile plants that can be used imaginatively all around the garden. The following pages show some of the interesting and beautiful ways in which roses can be used.

Some rose enthusiasts prefer to create a rose garden in which few other plants feature, but there is a risk that such a strategy will leave the garden looking bare and boring for a large part of the year. Others are put off planting more roses simply because of the short period of interest with some types, especially the once-flowering climbers and ramblers and some of the species and old-fashioned roses. By using roses imaginatively, however, it is possible to enjoy all their charm and beauty without sacrificing any of the delights of your garden.

PREVIOUS PAGE: Rosa 'Fantin Latour'.

ABOVE: Use climbers and ramblers to clothe otherwise boring fences and walls: even when flowering is over, the foliage will act as a pleasing green screen for the rest of summer and into autumn. Here 'Madame Alfred Carrière', which continues to flower intermittently into the autumn, is doing a magnificent job enhancing a boundary.

ABOVE: Plant roses in mixed borders, just like any other desirable flowering shrub. Here the yellow floribunda 'Chinatown' looks perfectly in place.

LEFT: Roses can soften and disguise harsh structures like the garden shed. This is the fragrant and almost thornless 'Blush Rambler'.

ABOVE: *Small trees can make excellent supports for climbers and ramblers. In this instance, the rambler 'Bobbie James' gives an apple tree a second flush of blossom.*

Purists may prefer their roses unadulterated, but most gardeners appreciate other plants too and one plant can often be used to enhance another. A rambling rose such as 'Wedding Day' climbing through a flowering cherry will drape the branches with creamy white flowers a month or two after the cherry blossom is over – giving two displays instead of one. A late-flowering clematis growing though a climbing or rambling rose will double the flowering capacity of a given space. Anyone with a strong sense of colour co-ordination might like to plant a clematis that flowers at the same time as the rose, creating an even more stunning effect. Prune the clematis back hard in early spring.

Roses can be used along with other shrubs in shrub or mixed borders, or used as hedges, flowering ground cover, or even as container plants. In recent years, breeders have created more versatile varieties with a much wider range of uses as well as longer flowering periods, opening up many possibilities for using them all around the garden.

ABOVE: *The clever positioning of a rose with an ornament or urn can lend structure to the planting and give a pleasing contrast of form. This is 'Golden Celebrations', a modern shrub.*

ABOVE: *Shrub roses look perfectly in place in a shrub or mixed border, and ramblers, climbers or pillar roses can be grown up supports to give height to the border.*

LEFT: *Roses can make charming container plants, but they must have an adequate volume of soil, and regular watering in dry weather is essential.*

HAPPY MARRIAGES

For some stunning effects, try interplanting your roses with other plants that make happy combinations of colour and form. Purists may consider this detracts from the roses, but as a garden feature roses can be enhanced by what you plant with them.

Pansies provide a simple solution if you just want to cover the ground between the roses, especially in winter and spring when the roses are not in leaf. In summer they will find it difficult to compete in the shade except at the edge of the border. Polyanthus are also useful for spring colour.

In summer, when the roses are in bloom, their companions need to be stronger and bolder plants. Annual grasses are easily planted among existing roses, but choose a variety of grass that does not grow taller than the rose. Lavenders and catmints (nepetas), with their blue, lavender or purple flowers, are popular companions, but these are permanent features in the bed and the spacing of the roses should allow for both plants.

ABOVE: *Lavenders and roses make pleasing companions, and offer a double dose of fragrance. This is* Lavandula angustifolia *acting as a pleasing backdrop for a pink rose.*

ABOVE: *Shrub roses and even ramblers are ideal for mixed borders if they can be given space to grow to their full potential. In this mainly white border, the white ramblers 'Félicité et Perpétue', 'Bobbie James' and 'Adélaïde d'Orléans' blend in beautifully among the other plants.*

It is worth experimenting with the unlikely, such as yellow day lilies (hemerocallis) with yellow roses or pink gypsophila interplanted among pink roses.

Always bear in mind that for tip-top roses you will need to feed, spray and, with some roses, regularly dead-head, so plants that make rose cultivation difficult may mean a sacrifice of quality of bloom.

RIGHT: Blues and reds or blues and pinks look good together, and the small flowers of catmints (nepetas) create a wash of background colour without competing with the roses.

BELOW: Feathery ornamental grasses make striking companions, softening the stiff starkness of the rose stems and bringing a sense of movement as they sway in the wind.

ABOVE: Clematis make ideal partners for roses, and here one acts as a bridge between 'Madame Alfred Carrière' and 'Bobbie James'. Clematis can be chosen to flower at the same time or to extend the period of interest by blooming later. If the clematis is to grow through the rose itself, where its stems will become entwined, selecting a late-flowering variety that needs cutting back hard in early spring will make the task of pruning more practicable.

BEAUTIFUL BEDS

Many roses, especially hybrid teas and floribundas, look best when massed in a rose bed. Where space is unrestricted, whole beds of a single variety can look stunning, especially when fragrance matches the perfection of bloom. Beds of mixed roses can also be very pleasing, but for impact plant in groups of about five plants of each variety and select varieties that harmonize well in terms of size and habit as well as colour.

Rose beds are most appropriate in a formal rose garden, with rectangular or circular beds set into the lawn, ideally with pergolas or arches clothed with climbers and ramblers. This kind of garden is a rose-lover's paradise, especially if it is set with suitably positioned seats surrounded by fragrance. Many enthusiasts willingly forego other plants for such bliss and beauty.

Floribundas are ideal for beds designed to be viewed from a distance, where a mass of blooms over a long period is more important than the quality of individual flowers. Beds of hybrid tea roses generally have less impact from a distance, and flowering can be more uneven, especially where there are many varieties in the same bed. This is irrelevant for those rose lovers who prefer to savour the beauty of individual blooms.

Many modern gardens are too small for formal rose beds set in a large lawn, but there is plenty of

ABOVE: A formal rose garden is the ideal way to grow roses. Both visual impact and scent are concentrated, and it is a magical place to sit on a hot summer's day. Large rose beds like these have space for many different kinds of rose, but even in a small rose garden it is important to use pergolas or frames for climbers to provide the essential element of height.

scope for patio beds. Choose low-growing floribunda varieties (sometimes described as patio roses) for small beds set into the patio. Patio and miniature roses are also ideal for raised beds, where they can replace seasonal bedding plants. Although the initial investment is greater, the money you save on seasonal bedding will recover the cost of the roses over a few seasons.

TOP RIGHT: Part of the famous Royal National Rose Society garden at Chiswell Green, near St Albans, Hertfordshire. This is one of the finest rose gardens in England, where rose beds abound and you can assess a wide range of varieties in a garden setting.

RIGHT: Rose beds have more impact if they are densely planted. The pink rose in the foreground of this picture is 'The Fairy', a polyantha rose.

$\mathcal{B}$ORDER BEAUTIES

$\mathcal{R}$oses are ideal border plants, whether in mixed plantings, or in a border dedicated to roses. Many varieties have a long flowering season that will out-perform most other flowering shrubs . . . and of course they contribute the special charm of their perfume.

If space rules out formal rose beds cut into the lawn, it is usually possible to create a rose border. Instead of filling it with herbaceous plants, pack it with roses of all kinds and colours. It will look spectacular in early and mid-summer, and will continue to offer pockets of interest right through until autumn.

Use shrub roses and pillar roses at the back of the border, modern shrub roses and the taller floribundas towards the centre, and compact floribundas and hybrid teas towards the front, with some of the long-flowering ground cover roses as an edging. A kaleidoscope of colour works best with this kind of rose border, and enables many varieties to be grown.

Rose borders are ideal for old-fashioned and modern shrub roses, many of which are too tall or bushy for formal rose beds. These roses also have a more informal shape more appropriate for a shrub border.

Use shrub roses to transform an existing shrub border that looks tired and boring, perhaps with large shrubs at the back that are mainly grown for their foliage. Shrub roses planted in front of large established shrubs will bring the border to life in summer, and the foliage behind makes a pleasing backdrop against which to view the roses. Species roses, especially the tall-growing kinds such as *Rosa moyesii*, grown for its decorative hips, and *R. sericea omeiensis pteracantha*, grown mainly for its spectacular thorns, are also ideal in this situation.

If there is no space for a formal rose garden or a rose border, integrate as many roses as possible into a mixed border. If you can make the border a viewpoint from an arbour of roses, or a sitting area framed by roses, so much the better.

ABOVE: *Use ramblers, climbers and other tall roses at the back of a rose border. This takes the eye right to the back of the border and the extra height ensures the feature is a focal point even from a distance.*

LEFT: *A plain dark green hedge makes a good background which to view a rose border. Pale colours like this 'Dapple Dawn', a shrub rose, show up particularly well.*

BELOW: *Try to incorporate a sitting area where you can linger to admire your rose border. Frame it with fragrant roses, perhaps using climbing roses to create a sense of enclosure like this. Use roses as a unifying theme to link different parts of the garden.*

OLD-FASHIONED CHARM

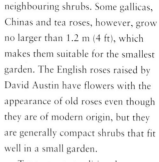

The *grandes dames* of the summer border, unsurpassed for their sumptuous flowers and heady fragrance, old roses still have a place in every garden. That they have endured so long is thanks not only to their beauty but also in many cases to their ease of cultivation.

Old roses lend themselves to an informal, mixed, cottage style of planting that also uses other shrubs, hardy perennials and summer bulbs. Many make large, spreading plants that need some form of support, though you can allow them to flop gracefully over and through

neighbouring shrubs. Some gallicas, Chinas and tea roses, however, grow no larger than 1.2 m (4 ft), which makes them suitable for the smallest garden. The English roses raised by David Austin have flowers with the appearance of old roses even though they are of modern origin, but they are generally compact shrubs that fit well in a small garden.

Try to create traditional cottage-garden groupings with old roses in mixed borders. The geometric shapes of alliums such as *A. sphaerocephalon* and *A. giganteum* are the perfect foil to the lax habit of many shrub roses, as are the strong verticals of foxgloves (*Digitalis purpurea*). The white or apricot-pink forms of the digitalis, or the milky blue or white Canterbury bell (*Campanula medium*), are particularly effective, and both are biennials easily raised from seed. The perennial *Campanula lactiflora* also works well.

For a less spiky, more integrated effect, use easy border perennials such as hardy geraniums, lady's mantle (*Alchemilla mollis*) or catmint (*Nepeta* x *faassenii*), all of which blend with most other plants. Clouds of perennial gypsophila (*G. paniculata*) or bronze fennel (*Foeniculum vulgare* 'Purpureum') will further soften the edges.

LEFT: *Lavender and lady's mantle (*Alchemilla mollis*) are perfect partners for old-fashioned roses and shrub roses of all kinds.*

Grey-leaved plants always look good with the soft pinks and crimsons of old roses. Try *Artemisia lactiflora*, lamb's ears (*Stachys byzantina*), and *Senecio* (now more correctly *Brachyglottis*) 'Sunshine'. The latter has yellow daisy flowers in summer, but you can remove these to prevent them clashing with the roses.

Underplant tall roses with something to clothe the ground, such as hostas, lavender, or the grey-leaved curry plant (*Helichrysum italicum*). The last two will only do well in a sunny position, however, whereas the hostas tolerate shade.

A SCENTED BORDER

Roses are indispensable for a scented border. To create a pot-pourri of scents, provide a backdrop of mock orange (philadelphus), the flowering of which will coincide with the roses' main mid-summer flush. Underplant with old-fashioned pinks such as the clove-scented 'Gran's Favourite', and try to include the heady fragrance of *Lilium regale* or the incense-scented ornamental tobacco *Nicotiana alata*.

ABOVE: Old roses like this gallica 'Duc de Guiche', known since 1835, are perfect for shrub and rose borders in the modern garden.

ABOVE: Rosa moyesii *is an invaluable species rose to grow among old-fashioned roses in the border. In summer its attractive single red flowers (left) are a feature, while autumn brings a bonus of stems festooned with flagon-shaped hips (right).*

LEFT: Including some species roses with decorative hips will prolong the period of interest. Rosa pimpinellifolia, *sometimes catalogued under its older name of* R. spinosissima, *is the Scotch or Burnet rose, with cream, white or pink flowers and very dark hips that eventually become almost black.*

HEDGES AND BOUNDARIES

Garden walls and fences are essentially functional: they are there to define the boundaries, to keep children and pets in and intruders out. For a rose lover they are also a wonderful opportunity to plant more roses.

Walls and fences represent golden opportunities for planting climbing and rambling roses. Climbers can be planted against tall walls, while ramblers are a better choice for lower walls and fences. However, even tall climbers and ramblers will spread horizontally along a fence if they cannot grow upwards.

Fix horizontal supports about 45–60 cm (1½–2 ft) apart, and train as many shoots as possible along these. New shoots will grow from this framework of horizontal branches to cover most of the wall or fence, whereas if all the shoots are allowed to grow upwards most of the flowers will be bunched together at the top and then simply tumble down over each other.

A Thorny Question

Rose hedges must not become neglected, especially those that border a public footpath. Overgrown roses with thorny shoots that catch on passers-by soon lead to disputes. If necessary, plant a little further into the garden and not right at the edge, so that they do not overhang the path.

ABOVE: 'Albertine', one of the all-time favourites among ramblers, looks wonderful growing against a tall boundary wall. It flowers prolifically and fills the air with scent. Only a susceptibility to mildew mars this choice: this will be less of a problem if it is grown over an openwork fence.

BELOW: Brick walls make an ideal background against which to view climbing roses, and in return the flowers soften the harshness of too much brickwork.

A ROSE HEDGE

Roses can make beautiful boundaries, and are ideal for an internal dividing hedge within the garden, but they will not provide the sense of privacy that, say, a privet or yew hedge can impart. Although thorny stems will deter intruders and some animals, a rose hedge is best regarded as an ornamental feature. It will be informal in profile, and should not be clipped to a neat outline with shears.

Given these limitations, roses can make some of the best flowering hedging, blooming for far longer than most shrubs – sometimes with the bonus of scent. Few other hedges can match the rose for colour, length of flowering period, and fragrance.

Traditional choices are *Rosa rugosa* and its varieties such as 'Scabrosa', or the hybrid musks 'Cornelia' and 'Penelope'. All these will make a hedge 1.2 m (4 ft) or more tall. For a lower hedge try 'Ballerina', a lower-growing hybrid musk with white flowers flushed pink. The hydrangea-like clusters of musk-scented flowers bloom over a long period.

Tall floribunda roses also make pretty hedges, though they are less substantial than the shrub roses already mentioned. For that reason it is best to plant them in a double staggered row. Pleasing varieties for this purpose are 'Eye Paint' (red with a white centre), 'Margaret Merril' (white), 'Masquerade' (multi-coloured) and 'Southampton' (apricot-orange).

ABOVE: A living wall of roses can make a delightful garden boundary. Even grown over quite a flimsy frame of trelliswork or chain link, roses soon provide dense cover that gives a sense of privacy in summer.

RIGHT: A covering of roses can make even the oldest of fences look attractive and act as a further barrier.

LEFT: Part of a rose hedge using 'Hansa', one of the rugosa hybrids.

CARPETS OF COLOUR

Roses sound unpromising as ground cover plants, but there are varieties able to create a carpet of colour that will look beautiful all summer long. They could transform an area of neglected ground or perhaps a steep bank that is difficult to cultivate.

Some of the older ground cover roses can be disappointing: they can be too tall for a small area and their flowering season is sometimes short. These criticisms cannot be levelled against many of the compact ground cover roses bred in recent years: they literally form a carpet of bloom.

Roses will not form an impenetrable barrier against weeds like some of the more traditional evergreen ground cover shrubs, but weeds are least active while the roses are dormant and devoid of foliage,

so they can be quite effective weed suppressers if the ground is cleared of weeds first and then mulched. The best way to be sure of eliminating weeds is to plant the roses through a mulching sheet.

The term "ground cover rose" is used to describe varieties with very different habits: some are ground-hugging while others are relatively tall and arching. Some have a spread of about 60 cm (2 ft) while others may reach 3 m (10 ft) or more across. If you are considering a ground cover rose, always make certain that its size and growth habit are what you want. All have their place in the garden, but the right kind must be chosen for each situation.

These are the broad groups into which most ground cover roses fit, though a few fall between these broad brushstroke headings:

Tall ground cover roses with arching stems include 'Pink Bells' and 'Red Bells', which grow little more than 1 m (3 ft) tall but have a spread of about 1.2 m (4 ft) or more. The plants are smothered in double flowers in mid- and late summer. Prune them like shrub roses, but concentrate on shortening any branches which want to grow vertically.

ABOVE: 'Pink Bells', one of the larger ground cover roses, reaches about 1.2 m (4 ft), but it is a real eye-catcher where there is space for it.

ABOVE: 'Suffolk' is one of the brightest ground cover roses. It grows about 45 cm (1½ ft) tall and has a spread of about 1 m (3 ft).

LEFT: 'Essex' has spreading shoots that make a plant about 1.2 m (4 ft) wide.

Tall ground cover roses that are about as wide as they are tall include 'Rosy Cushion' (pink, single), 'Smarty' (rose-madder, single), 'Surrey' (pink, double, very long-flowering), and 'Sussex' (apricot-buff, double, with a long flowering season). Prune them like those with arching stems.

Ground-hugging varieties which spread wider than their height and usually creep along the ground include 'Flower Carpet' (bright pink, double, blooming over a very long period), 'Grouse' (pale pink, single flowers in mid- and late summer; less than 30 cm (1 ft) tall, but spreads to about 3 m (10 ft) across), 'Kent' (white, semi-double), 'Max Graf' (pink, single, grows to about 1.8 m (6ft) across), 'Nozomi' (white flushed pink, single), 'Pheasant' (pink, double, flowers in mid- and late summer, with a 3 m (10 ft) spread) and 'Snow Carpet' (white, double). All these require minimal pruning other than to shorten the longest stems to restrain their spread.

TOP RIGHT: 'Flower Carpet' is an outstanding variety with large, very bright blooms produced all summer and even into autumn.

MIDDLE RIGHT: A traditional ground cover rose, 'Grouse' lacks the brightness of many newer varieties but is useful for clothing a bank.

RIGHT: 'Nozomi' is sometimes classified as a climbing miniature, but unsupported it forms a ground cover shrub about 1.2 m (4 ft) across.

PLANTING GROUND COVER ROSES

Although ground cover roses will help to suppress weeds once they are well established, for real maintenance-free beds they should be planted through a sheet mulch.

Sheet mulches will not add nutrients to the soil or improve its structure as many organic "loose" mulches do, so thorough ground preparation is essential. Always incorporate plenty of humus-forming material such as garden compost or well-rotted manure, and rake in a balanced fertilizer if preparing the ground in spring, or a controlled-release fertilizer or bonemeal for autumn or winter planting.

2 Make cross-shaped planting slits in the sheet with a knife or scissors. If the rose's root-ball is large it may be necessary to make the slits large enough to take a spade, but the flaps can still simply be folded back into place afterwards.

3 Roses in a small container can be planted with a trowel, but a spade may be needed for large ones. Provided the ground was well prepared before the sheet was laid, it should be easy to dig out the planting hole.

1 Always prepare the ground thoroughly before laying the mulching sheet. Make a slit around the edge of the bed with a spade, and push the sheet into this. Firm the soil around the edge to ensure the sheet is held taut over the bed.

4 If the roses are already planted, but not too large, the sheet can be applied by making large slits at the positions of the plants, then slipping it over them. Simply fold the flaps back around the stems – it will not matter if the join is not perfect as it can be covered with a decorative mulch.

5 Although most of the sheet mulch will be hidden as the plants grow, initially it will be very conspicuous. A layer of a decorative mulch such as chipped bark or gravel will make it much more acceptable.

6 *(Right)* An inexpensive plastic mulch can be used for newly planted ground cover roses with a view to removing it once the plants are well established. Its appearance can be improved by covering it with chipped bark – as only a thin layer is required to hide the sheet, this should be cheaper than using a thick layer of chipped bark on its own.

Which Material?

Black polythene (plastic) is inexpensive and widely available. It does not allow water to penetrate, so it is best used in narrow strips, perhaps on either side of a newly planted rose hedge.

Woven plastic mulches are more expensive, but they allow water to seep through while suppressing weeds by keeping out the light.

There are a few sheet mulches that are made from biodegradable materials such as wool waste. This is a good option if the sheet mulch is required only while the roses are becoming established.

RIGHT: *'Pink Bells' makes suitable ground cover in a large garden.*

CLIMBERS AND RAMBLERS

There are few more idyllic images than that of a country cottage in high summer, the garden gate arched over and the house walls wreathed with roses. Not everyone has that kind of setting, but climbers and ramblers can be just as beautiful in a small modern town garden, if planted with imagination.

A climbing or rambling rose will lend an air of maturity and timelessness even to the most modern home. Try planting one of the heavily scented varieties such as 'Albertine', 'New Dawn' or 'Zéphirine Drouhin' by the front door, perhaps trained against a trellis. 'Zéphirine Drouhin' is a particularly useful variety for this position because it has no thorns to catch on clothing.

Climbing roses have a number of other uses in the garden. Where there is space, you could allow a climber or rambler to grow with the minimum of pruning to produce a huge fountain of flowers. The rambling 'Albertine' grown in this way would make a magnificent spectacle.

Climbing roses are also suitable for growing against pillars and pergolas. Rustic poles are appropriate in cottage gardens, although brick pillars are more substantial and permanent supports.

Some varieties can also be trained along ropes slung between two supports to create a flowering bower at the back of a border. For this purpose, choose a medium-growing

Mask the Bare Bits

Climbing roses tend to become bare at the base in time, so mask this by underplanting with easy perennials such as catmint (nepeta), lamb's ears (*Stachys byzantina*), lady's mantle (*Alchemilla mollis*) or hostas.

ABOVE: *Roses scrambling over an archway are quintessential ingredients of a country garden, though you can achieve a similar effect in an enclosed town garden too. As well as bringing a delightful froth of blooms high above the path, the archway creates a simple screening effect that offers an illusion of space.*

variety with long flexible stems, such as 'Madame Grégoire Staechelin', that can be looped around the rope to make swags of flowers.

Pillars, pyramids or tripods placed towards the back of the border can be covered with shorter-growing varieties such as 'Golden Showers' or 'Handel', or one of the Bourbon roses such as 'Madame Isaac Pereire' or 'Louise Odier'.

Free-standing trellis panels can be used to train the roses to, and they look particularly pleasing if painted white or in a colour that enhances the variety you are growing.

Very vigorous climbers, some of which can reach 10 m (30 ft) or more with a suitable support, are best accommodated by planting them where they can grow into a tree. 'Seagull' and 'Wedding Day' are among the varieties suitable for this.

Rambling roses can be grown informally by allowing them to scramble through large shrubs such as lilacs that are dull after their show of flowers in late spring or early summer. You can also plant them where they will trail over a fence to make a "curtain" of flowers.

ABOVE: If you have a pretty window like this, make the most of it by framing it with a climbing rose.

ABOVE: Be bold: try colour-coordinating your fence and roses. This pastel pink fence perfectly matches the climbing rose behind.

ABOVE: Climbing versions of hybrid tea and floribunda roses are best grown against a trellis on a wall or pillar. This is 'Climbing Iceberg'.

LEFT: Conifers do not make ideal supports for vigorous climbing or rambling roses, as they tend to cling to the surface instead of growing through the branches, but 'Seagull' is happy scaling the heights here.

RIGHT: Wooden pyramids or tripods make a solid support for climbers planted at the back of a border. This variety is 'Louise Odier'.

PLANTING A WALL CLIMBER

Roses need special care when planted against a wall, where a "rain shadow" means the soil is often dry. A decorative trellis will improve air circulation and help to make a feature of the new rose while it is becoming established.

A large trellis makes an attractive support for small climbers, though it is also possible to support them by means of galvanized or plastic-covered wire stretched between vine eyes fixed to the wall.

To ensure adequate air circulation between the plant and the wall, mount the trellis on battens. This also makes it easier to remove the plant if you need to paint or repair the wall.

Whichever method of support is chosen, take trouble over planting the rose, and be prepared to water it regularly during the first season. Even after rain the soil close to a house wall can be dry.

2 Screw the battens to the wall.

3 Nail the trellis to the battens.

4 Fork over the planting area, working in plenty of organic matter – in this case, spent mushroom compost. If the area is paved it may be necessary to remove some of the paving first.

1 Decide on the best position for the trellis on the wall, then drill holes at suitable intervals to take the battens. Tap in plastic wall plugs to take the screws.

5 Dig the planting hole at least 30 cm (1 ft) from the wall, and twice the depth and width of the container or roots. Fork in more organic matter and a handful of bonemeal or balanced fertilizer.

6 *(Left)* Check the planting depth, and adjust if necessary by adding or removing soil until the level is as required.

7 Remove the rose from its pot and gently tease out a few roots from around the edge of the root-ball to encourage the rose to root into the surrounding soil more quickly.

8 Position the rose in the hole, angling the top growth towards the wall. If planting a bare-root rose, fan the roots out away from the wall, to ensure they receive adequate moisture. Backfill with soil.

9 Firm the soil with your foot to ensure the rose is firmly planted and there are no large air pockets in which the roots might dry out.

10 Cut back any dead or damaged growth, but leave longer, healthy stems unpruned. Also remove any faded flowers.

11 If they are long enough, fan out the stems and tie them loosely to the trellis.

12 Finally, water in thoroughly. If planting in spring, fork a little rose or general balanced fertilizer around the base of the plant, at the rate recommended by the manufacturer. The rose should establish quickly and soon produce vigorous shoots that can be trained to the trellis.

ℛAISING STANDARDS

*S*tandard roses lend height to rose beds and act as focal points, but they can be used just as effectively in summer bedding schemes and as container plants on the patio.

Roses grown as standards inevitably become focal points in a way that an individual bush rose seldom can. Not only are they raised above most of the other roses, they have an "architectural" shape that simply demands attention. For that reason a single specimen in the centre of a formal flower bed is often the centre of attention, and when planted in a rose bed a single plant can compete with perhaps dozens of lower-growing hybrid teas or floribundas in visual terms.

Be cautious when planting standards among other roses. Standards come in different heights (see box) and the impact will be lost if a small standard is planted among tall bush roses.

Standards are not specific varieties, but ordinary bush varieties budded on to a long stem, which makes it possible to plant bush and standard forms of the same variety – say standard and bush forms of 'Iceberg' in an all-white bed. For a less subtle and more dazzling effect, choose a contrasting colour.

Weeping standards are varieties of ramblers. The stems cascade and are sometimes trained over an umbrella-like frame, though many experts do not approve of these and consider

ABOVE: *An uncommon variety, 'Centenaire de Lourdes' is a floribunda that makes a spectacular standard.*

LEFT: *Patio standards are becoming popular, especially for small gardens where space is limited. Here 'Sweet Dream' brings a breath of beauty by the front door – a lovely welcome for visitors.*

that the stems look better if allowed to cascade naturally. In either case weeping standards will produce a curtain of colour, with stems that often cascade to ground level. Ground cover roses, such as 'Grouse' and 'Nozomi', are also used to produce weeping standards, and even shrub roses with arching stems, such as 'Ballerina' and 'Canary Bird', can be obtained in this form.

Weeping roses almost always look best as specimen plants in a lawn, where their symmetry and beauty can be fully appreciated.

Patio standards are usually dwarf floribundas on stems about 75 cm (2½ ft) tall, and these look great by the front door or in a light porch, as well as on the patio.

BELOW LEFT: A well-grown weeping standard has evenly spaced shoots all around the head, cascading almost to ground level.

BELOW RIGHT: The rambler 'Excelsa' makes a superb weeping standard that is always an eye-catcher.

BOTTOM RIGHT: 'American Pillar' is more often seen growing over pergolas, but it also makes a pleasing standard.

How Tall?

Standards vary in height. Although different growers may use slightly different terminology and sizes, these are typical stem heights (the actual head may increase the total height):

Miniature standard: 45 cm (1 ½ ft)
Half standard: 75 cm (2 ½ ft)
Patio standard: 75 cm (2 ½ ft)
Full standard: 1 m (3 ft)
Weeping standard:
    1.2–1.5 m (4–5 ft)

PERFECTION IN MINIATURE

Miniatures are tiny, scaled-down roses, perfect for those who enjoy the exquisite beauty of tiny plants, or who simply do not have the space for full-sized roses.

Most miniatures are small versions of hybrid tea and floribunda roses, though a few climbers are also classified as miniature.

Miniatures are widely sold as pot plants, but they are unsuitable for a permanent place indoors. They are best planted in the garden when the initial display is over, but they must first be carefully hardened off. If you are buying miniature roses with the garden in mind, choose those sold for the purpose, whether from a garden centre or by mail order.

As with full-sized roses, some varieties are more vigorous and taller than others: the larger ones may be too big for a miniature rose garden but very suitable for raised beds and other uses.

ABOVE: Miniatures are often sold as pot plants, but they can only be kept indoors for a short period before they begin to deteriorate. Tiny miniatures like this could look lost in a bed outdoors.

While the tiniest varieties grow to only about 15 cm (6 in), most miniatures are 20–30 cm (8–12 in) tall, while the larger ones reach 30–38 cm (12–15 in). A few, such as 'Peek A Boo', border on being a patio rose, and you may find such borderline varieties classed as either miniatures or patio roses in different catalogues.

USING MINIATURE ROSES

A few enthusiasts build rose gardens in miniature, complete with scaled-down beds, paths and lawns. This often appeals to model-makers and rose enthusiasts with little more than a small backyard or balcony. Miniatures are far more versatile than this, however, and they have a role to play even in a large garden.

In a small garden, miniatures and patio roses can replace full-sized versions if the desire is for a collection of many different varieties – though beware of planting a bed with individual specimens of dozens of different roses: plant at least five of one variety to make an impact. A whole bed of one miniature variety will have much more impact than a medley of different ones, as they will probably vary in height and habit as well as colour.

Raised beds, whether on the patio or elsewhere, are the ideal home for miniature roses. They are closer to eye level, and the beauty of their individual flowers can be appreciated.

Miniatures make pleasing outdoor table decorations for, say, a patio table. They can also be used in window boxes, tubs and troughs, but they do not mix well with summer bedding plants, which tend to swamp them. Pack your containers with miniature or patio roses.

LEFT: Beds of miniature roses can be very pleasing, but lots of plants are required to achieve the same kind of impact as far fewer full-sized floribunda roses.

ᴀᴀʙᴏᴠᴇ: *Try miniatures in pots and contain-ers for the patio.*

ʟᴇꜰᴛ: *Raised beds are ideal for miniature roses, which are thus brought closer to eye level.*

Explore possibilities in the rock garden. To some, a rose will seem alien among true alpines, but in a rock garden where many different kinds of plants are grown, miniature roses will bring summer colour after most traditional rock plants have passed their best. Choose real dwarfs or the taller miniatures according to the space available and the scale of the rock garden.

STANDARDS AND CLIMBERS

Miniature standards are available, but for a general garden display they may not have any more impact than the ordinary bush forms – which are also less expensive. Standards come into their own as part of a miniature version of a full-sized rose garden, planted along with the bush forms.

"Miniature climber" is a potentially misleading term. Although small in comparison with normal climbers, they are not necessarily in scale with the bush forms. In general, they are best regarded as small climbers suitable for the patio or other areas where space is restricted.

ᴀʙᴏᴠᴇ: *Miniature roses can be planted in the rock garden, where they will bring colour at a time when it is scarce among the alpines.*

ʟᴇꜰᴛ: *Miniature standards are best grown among bush miniatures, where they look in scale and are easily seen.*

$\mathcal{P}$OTTED PLEASURES

$\mathcal{D}$o not dismiss the idea of roses as container plants. Pots and tubs enable roses to be grown in parts of the garden that would otherwise be bereft of them, and in some town gardens it is the *only* way it is possible to grow them.

Most kinds of rose can be grown in a container provided it is large enough. Except in the case of miniatures, this means a half-barrel, shrub tub, or large pot with a diameter of *at least* 30 cm (12 in) and preferably 45 cm (18 in). As the rose will remain in its container for many years, it is worth investing in an ornamental container that looks decorative in its own right. It will enhance the beauty of the rose and look more pleasing in winter when the rose is dormant.

Decide on the final position of the container before planting, as once finished it will be very heavy to move.

WHAT TO GROW

Patio roses (dwarf floribundas) are showy and easy to grow, but full-sized floribundas and hybrid teas can be grown if the container is large enough. Unfortunately, the latter look inelegant when dormant and are best positioned where they can be appreciated in summer but are not too dominant in winter. A rose of a pale colour such as white or yellow

will show up superbly against a hedge or wall when in flower, while in winter the bare stems will not be too obtrusive. However, hybrid teas would not be a good choice to grow by the front door.

Rather than grow a bush form of a hybrid tea or floribunda, consider a standard. These make impressive container plants and can become useful focal points.

ABOVE: *Floribundas like 'The Times Rose' can make imposing container plants, but they must be pruned thoroughly and watered and fed as necessary.*

LEFT: *Miniatures are some of the best roses for containers. This is 'Sunny Sunblaze'.*

BELOW: *'Flower Carpet' is an outstanding patio or ground cover rose. This plant was still in flower in late autumn in its year of planting.*

Small patio roses and miniatures can be grown in smaller containers that are easily moved to a less conspicuous spot in the garden for the dormant season.

In general, shrub roses are too large and loose in their growth habit to make perfect container plants, but some of the English roses, such as 'Evelyn', or dainty tea or China roses, are sufficiently compact to be grown in a half-barrel.

Climbers are sometimes planted in large containers, perhaps if they have to climb against a wall where there is no soil in which to plant them. Small climbers, such as 'Warm Welcome' and 'Nozomi', can be planted in free-standing containers supported by a tepee of canes.

Watering and Feeding

Containers will require daily watering at the height of summer, possibly twice a day in very hot weather. This is a job for the cool of evening, when less water will be lost through evaporation.

To maintain vigour in subsequent years after planting, top-dress with bonemeal or work in a rose fertilizer at the rate recommended by the manufacturer each spring.

Supplementary feeding will be necessary for vigorous plants, particularly climbers, and a foliar or liquid feed will be quick-acting and provide the necessary boost. Do not feed after midsummer, however, as sappy growth that has not ripened fully will be vulnerable to winter frost damage.

LEFT: 'Nozomi' is an extremely versatile rose that takes readily to life in a container. Unless it is trained up a support, it will spread and cascade and completely hide the container in a surprisingly short time. This specimen has been planted only a couple of months yet is already well established in its plastic shrub tub.

BELOW: 'Nozomi' shows its versatility again, this time growing from a half-basket fixed to the house wall. Some other ground cover roses can be grown in a similar way.

BOTTOM: The pure white floribunda 'Iceberg' brings light to a dull corner, and is perfectly happy in its large container.

PLANTING A ROSE IN A CONTAINER

Some roses will do well in containers, but they require careful planting to get them off to a good start and provide conditions that will sustain them in future years.

1 Cover the base of a half-barrel or large pot with stones or gravel for drainage and to provide stability, then part-fill the container with a loam-based potting soil. This will have a better reserve of nutrients and give greater stability than a peat or peat-substitute mixture.

2 Check the planting depth while the rose is still in its container. The top of the root-ball should be about 2.5 cm (1 in) below the rim of the container, to allow for watering.

4 Set the rose in position in the centre of the container and backfill with the potting soil.

3 Ease the rose out of its container and carefully tease out some of the roots to encourage them to grow out into the surrounding soil.

5 Once the correct level has been reached, firm the potting soil to remove any large pockets of air where the roots could dry out.

6 Water the rose thoroughly. To improve its appearance, sprinkle fine gravel, stone chippings or chipped bark over the surface. This will also reduce evaporation from the soil.

Supporting a Climber

To support a climber in a free-standing container, insert about five canes (an odd number looks best), pushing them to the bottom for stability. Tie the tops of the canes together to create a "wigwam", then tie string or plastic-coated wire around the canes in loops about 20 cm (8 in) apart, or in a spiral as shown. Tie in the stems as they grow.

The following climbing and rambling roses are suitable for growing in containers: 'Casino', 'Céline Forestier', 'Climbing Orange Sunblaze', 'Dublin Bay', 'Golden Showers', 'Good as Gold', 'Laura Ford', 'Maigold', 'Nice Day', 'Phyllis Bide', 'Swan Lake', 'Warm Welcome', 'White Cockade'.

RIGHT: *With regular feeding and watering, a small climber will send up strong stems that can be trained into a permanent structure around cane supports.*

ROSE GALLERY

This gallery of roses contains just a small selection of the varieties that can be obtained from specialist rose nurseries and garden centres, and is intended to be a representative selection of roses new and old. If you have not planted roses before, use it to help you decide on the types of roses that appeal to you, but bear in mind that these are just a few of hundreds of excellent varieties available for your garden.

ℛAMBLERS AND CLIMBERS

'ALBERTINE' (RAMBLER)
Introduced in 1921, this is one of the best known of all ramblers, deservedly popular for its heavy scent, prolific flowering and lovely colour. The blooms become untidy as they pass their peak, and the variety is prone to mildew, but it is still an outstanding rose. Height: 4.5 m (15 ft). Spread: 3.5 m (12 ft).

'AMERICAN PILLAR' (RAMBLER)
Introduced in 1902, this used to be a very popular rose. It has fallen out of favour, perhaps because of its single flowers, lack of scent, and susceptibility to mildew. Despite these drawbacks, it is an eye-catching rose for a pillar or pergola, making an outstanding garden feature. Height: 4.5 m (15 ft). Spread: 2.4 m (8 ft).

'BOBBIE JAMES' (RAMBLER)
Introduced in 1961, this versatile but vigorous rambler looks good growing over a large pergola, on a large support at the back of a border, or scrambling into a tree. The cupped, white, semi-double flowers are small but borne in large trusses and sweetly scented. Height: 9 m (30 ft). Spread: 6 m (20 ft).

'CLIMBING ENA HARKNESS' (CLIMBER)
Introduced in 1954, it was a sport (mutation) from the then popular hybrid tea 'Ena Harkness'. It requires coaxing and does best in a warm, sheltered site, but it has the shape and scent of a classic rose. Height: 4.5 m (15 ft). Spread: 2.4 m (8 ft).

'DANSE DU FEU' (CLIMBER)
Introduced in 1954, and by modern standards prone to blackspot, this vivid rose is nevertheless very free-flowering and remains a popular climber. It flowers from summer to autumn, and the blooms are lightly scented. Height: 2.4 m (8 ft). Spread: 2.4 m (8 ft).

'DUBLIN BAY' (CLIMBER)
Introduced in 1976, this is an outstanding climber for a small garden. The lightly scented flowers are produced amid healthy, glossy leaves from summer to autumn. A good choice where a climber that is not too rampant is required. Height: 2.4 m (8 ft). Spread: 2.4 m (8 ft).

PREVIOUS PAGE: Rosa *'Graham Thomas'*.

'HANDEL' (CLIMBER)

Introduced in 1965, and a variety valued primarily for its unique colouring, this vigorous rose flowers from mid-summer to autumn. It is only lightly scented, and blackspot may be a problem, but the flowers stand up well to wet weather. Height: 3 m (10 ft). Spread: 2.1 m (7 ft).

'MADAME GRÉGOIRE STAECHELIN' (CLIMBER)

Introduced in 1927, but still grown for its sweetly scented warm pink flowers, borne in profusion in early summer. It flowers only once, but at its peak the display is superb, and there are large showy hips to redden in autumn. Height: 6 m (20 ft). Spread: 3.5 m (12 ft).

'MAIGOLD' (CLIMBER)

Introduced in 1954 and still widely planted, this is an outstanding rose valued for its disease resistance and early flowering (usually by late spring). Unfortunately it does not continue to flower through the summer. The leaves are leathery and glossy. Height: 2.4 m (8 ft). Spread: 2.4 m (8 ft).

'PARKDIREKTOR RIGGERS' (CLIMBER)

Introduced in 1957 but highly regarded for its disease resistance and long flowering season. The semi-double flowers are only lightly scented, but are produced from summer into autumn. It has glossy dark green leaves. Height: 3.5 m (12 ft). Spread: 2.4 m (8 ft).

'PINK PERPÉTUE' (CLIMBER)

Introduced in 1965, and a variety with exceedingly beautiful blooms, borne from summer to autumn, its spreading habit makes it suitable for covering a wall. The blooms are only lightly scented, and the leaves may succumb to rust. Height: 3 m (10 ft). Spread: 2.4 m (8 ft).

'WHITE COCKADE' (CLIMBER)

Introduced in 1969, it is still valued for its perfectly shaped flowers. The blooms are only slightly scented, but produced almost continuously from summer to autumn. It is a good choice for a container or for growing on a short pillar. Height: 2.1 m (7 ft). Spread: 1.5 m (5 ft).

FLORIBUNDA (CLUSTER-FLOWERED) ROSES

'ANISLEY DICKSON'

Introduced in 1985, and named after the breeder's wife – an indication of a good rose. It is a fine bedding rose and makes a pleasing hedge. It is only slightly fragrant, but with abundant foliage. Height: 1 m (3 ft). Spread: 60 cm (2 ft).

'ANNA LIVIA'

Introduced in 1988, this free-flowering variety is ideal for bedding, with fragrant, hybrid-tea-shaped blooms. Height: 75 cm (2½ ft). Spread: 60 cm (2 ft).

'BRIGHT SMILE'

Introduced in 1980, this is a fitting name for a cheerful yellow rose which flowers early and produces a good succession of bloom. Its low height and bushy growth make it suitable for the front of a border or as a low hedge. It shows good disease resistance. Slight fragrance. Height: 60 cm (2 ft). Spread: 45 cm (1½ ft).

'BUCK'S FIZZ'

Introduced in 1990. Though grown primarily for its soft orange colour, the blooms are also fragrant. Height: 1 m (3 ft). Spread: 60 cm (2 ft).

'CHAMPAGNE COCKTAIL'

Introduced in 1985, this showy rose is very decorative, free-flowering and shows very good disease resistance. It makes a colourful bed, and is also an attractive cut flower, with a strong scent for floribundas. Height: 1 m (3 ft). Spread: 60 cm (2 ft).

'COVENTRY CATHEDRAL'

Introduced in 1973, the colour makes this a real eye-catcher in full flower. Unfortunately it is susceptible to blackspot. Height: 75 cm (2½ ft). Spread: 60 cm (2 ft).

'ELIZABETH OF GLAMIS'
Introduced in 1964, and once a very popular rose with a good fragrance. By modern standards it is prone to diseases and dieback, but it is lovely when grown in good soil. Height: 75 cm (2½ ft). Spread: 60 cm (2 ft).

'EVELYN FISON'
Introduced in 1962, it became very popular and is still highly regarded. The colour is strong and does not fade even in the hottest sun. Slight fragrance. Height: 1 m (3 ft). Spread: 60 cm (2 ft).

'EYE PAINT'
Introduced in 1976, this is an exceptionally showy plant that stands out even when viewed across the garden. Its flowers are borne in great profusion, on a vigorous bush that grows larger than most floribundas. It looks at home in a shrub border, and makes an excellent informal hedge. There is no fragrance. Height: 1.2 m (4 ft). Spread: 75 cm (2½ ft).

'GLAD TIDINGS'
Introduced in 1989, when it was voted Rose of the Year. Good for beds, borders or an informal hedge, but only slightly fragrant. The flowers are produced in profusion and continue to flower over a long period. Height: 75 cm (2½ ft). Spread: 60 cm (2 ft).

'HANNAH GORDON'
Introduced in 1983. The delicately coloured flowers are well set off by the glossy bronze-green foliage. Height: 1 m (3 ft). Spread: 60 cm (2 ft).

'HARVEST FAYRE'
Introduced in 1990, when it won the Rose of the Year award. A bushy grower with large clusters of flowers late into the season. Some fragrance. Height: 1 m (3 ft). Spread: 60 cm (2 ft).

'ICEBERG'

Introduced in 1958, this is still one of the best white floribundas. The large flower clusters are borne in profusion, making it excellent for a massed effect or an informal hedge. It is also known by the name 'Schneewittchen'. Height: 1.2 m (4 ft). Spread: 60 cm (2 ft).

'MASQUERADE'

Introduced in 1949, and still one of the most easily identified roses. Although seldom planted now, its multicoloured effect still has appeal. There is only slight fragrance, and it requires regular dead-heading to keep the flowers coming. Height: 1 m (3 ft). Spread: 60 cm (2 ft).

'MATANGI'

Introduced in 1974, this is an eye-catching rose that produces a large profusion of flowers throughout the growing season, set off against glossy foliage. It is only slightly fragrant but it makes an excellent bedding rose and shows good disease resistance. Height: 75 cm (2½ ft). Spread: 60 cm (2 ft).

'MEMENTO'

Introduced in 1978. A very free-flowering rose with large trusses of blooms that continue to be produced throughout the season. The flowers are very weather-resistant and the plant's disease resistance is good too. There is only a trace of scent. Height: 75 cm (2 ½ ft). Spread: 60 cm (2 ft).

'MOUNTBATTEN'

Introduced in 1982, when it was Rose of the Year. The large, scented flowers show up well against the shiny foliage which is abundantly produced and persists well into winter. This variety is useful as an isolated shrub as well as in a rose bed or as an informal hedge. Height: 1 m (3 ft). Spread: 75 cm (2½ ft).

'QUAKER STAR'

Introduced in 1991. The medium-sized flowers remain beautifully shaped at all stages, from bud to fully open bloom. Only slightly fragrant. Height: 1 m (3 ft). Spread: 60 cm (2 ft).

'SHEILA'S PERFUME'
Introduced in 1985. Good perfumes are
not common among the floribundas, but
this one is very fragrant and it has won
awards for its scent. The flowers have long,
straight stems and are ideal for cutting.
Height: 1 m (3 ft). Spread: 60 cm (2 ft).

'STRAWBERRY ICE'
Introduced in 1979. The blooms have the
kind of delightful colour combination that
makes this rose difficult to ignore. It
makes a good show in the garden and is
great for cutting. Height: 1 m (3 ft).
Spread: 60 cm (2 ft).

'TANGO'
Introduced in 1989. The strikingly
coloured flowers are borne in great
profusion, but are only slightly fragrant.
An award-winning rose that deserves a
place in the garden. Height: 75 cm (2½
ft). Spread: 60 cm (2 ft).

'THE TIMES ROSE'
Introduced in 1984/5, this award-winning variety has a depth of colour that makes it an
impressive bedding rose. The dark green foliage increases the impression of substance.
Fragrance is only slight. Height: 1 m (3 ft). Spread: 60 cm (2 ft).

'VALENTINE HEART'
Introduced in 1990, this variety is aptly
named as it has a romantic appearance
and there is the bonus of a strong
perfume. The blooms are very weather-
tolerant, and the variety has justifiably
won several awards. Height: 1 m (3 ft).
Spread: 60 cm (2 ft).

GROUND COVER ROSES

'FERDY'
Introduced in 1984. An attractive shrub
with arching growth. Its height means it is
only suitable for ground cover in a large
garden. Height: 1.2 m (4 ft). Spread: 1 m
(3 ft).

'FIONA'
Introduced in 1979. A shrubby rose with
flower sprays borne throughout the
summer, set against plentiful dark green
glossy foliage. Height: 60 cm (2 ft).
Spread: 1.5 m (5 ft).

'GROUSE'
Introduced in 1984. A prostrate shrub
suitable for a bank or other large area.
The flowers are fragrant and the foliage
disease-resistant. Height: 30 cm (1 ft).
Spread: 3 m (10 ft).

'HERTFORDSHIRE'
Introduced in 1991. A ground-hugging
shrub with a profusion of bloom over a
very long flowering period. Height: 30 cm
(1 ft). Spread: 1 m (3 ft).

'NOZOMI'
Introduced in 1968, and bred in Japan. It
is a very versatile plant with many uses –
it will sometimes be found classified as a
miniature climber. Although the flowers
are not bright, they are borne in profusion
in mid-summer, and may go on appearing
into the autumn. Height: 30 cm (1 ft).
Spread: 1.2 m (4 ft).

'PINK BELLS'
Introduced in 1980, it has arching growth
with dark green shiny foliage that acts as
a pleasing backdrop for the pink flowers.
The slightly fragrant flowers are borne in
mid- and late summer. Its height means it
is only suitable for ground cover in a large
garden. Height: 75 cm (2½ ft). Spread:
1.2 m (4 ft).

'RED BELLS'
Introduced in 1983. A charming rose, similar to 'Pink Bells' (see previous page) apart from its colour. Height: 75 cm (2½ ft). Spread: 1.2 m (4 ft).

'RED MAX GRAF'
Introduced in 1984. A vigorous shrub with arching growth. It has one main flush of flowers in summer, but they are carried in profusion over dark green foliage. A good ground cover rose for a bank. Height: 45 cm (1½ ft). Spread: 1.5 m (5 ft).

'ROSY CUSHION'
Introduced in 1979. Good repeat flowering, and vigorous spreading growth with dense glossy foliage, but its height makes it unsuitable for areas requiring compact ground cover. Height: 1 m (3 ft). Spread: 1.2 m (4 ft).

'SNOW CARPET'
Introduced in 1980. A distinctive prostrate rose with creeping stems and a mass of tiny foliage to help smother weeds. Flowers for most of the summer and into the autumn. Height: 23 cm (9 in). Spread: 1 m (3 ft).

'THE FAIRY'
Introduced in 1932. A dwarf polyantha rose and one of the oldest ground cover roses, but still useful where there is space for it. Height: 75 cm (2½ ft). Spread: 1.2 m (4 ft).

HYBRID TEA (LARGE-FLOWERED) ROSES

'ALEXANDER'
Introduced in 1972, and still one of the best within its colour range. The long stems also make it a popular choice for cutting, and its size is suitable for hedging. Fragrance is only slight, but it holds many international awards. Height: 1.5 m (5 ft). Spread: 60 cm (2 ft).

'BLUE MOON'
Introduced in 1964, and popular because of its unusual colour and distinctive name, though it is a lilac-blue and not a true blue. The flowers are nicely pointed and have a good scent. It has reasonably good disease resistance. Height: 1 m (3 ft). Spread: 60 cm (2 ft).

'DAWN CHORUS'
Introduced in 1993, when its strong colour and good shape helped it win Rose of the Year and Breeder's Choice awards in that year. A free-flowering vigorous plant, it is ideal for rose beds, but its fragrance is only moderate. Height: 1 m (3 ft). Spread: 60 cm (2 ft).

'FULTON MACKAY'
Introduced in 1988, since when it has proved itself to be an excellent all-round rose. It has a sharp, spicy scent, weather resistance is good and the leaves are large and glossy. Height: 1 m (3 ft). Spread: 60 cm (2 ft).

'INGRID BERGMAN'
Introduced in 1986, and grown mainly for its strong colour and classic flower shape, though its fragrance is only light. The growth is strong and upright, with dark green glossy foliage, and it makes a good bedding rose. Height: 1 m (3 ft). Spread: 75 cm (2½ ft).

'JUST JOEY'
Introduced in 1973, but still grown for its distinctive colouring. The blooms are often large and it is always an eye-catching rose, but with only a slight scent. Its bushy growth makes it a good choice for a rose bed. Height: 75 cm (2½ ft). Spread: 60 cm (2 ft).

'KEEPSAKE'
Introduced in 1981. An attractive colour, good shape and sweet scent are its main attributes. It is a vigorous grower, with plenty of foliage. Height: 1.2 m (4 ft). Spread: 60 cm (2 ft).

'LOVELY LADY'
Introduced in 1986. A shapely, full-petalled rose with a pleasing fragrance. It looks especially good in a bed of a single variety. Height: 75 cm (2½ ft). Spread: 60 cm (2 ft).

'PAINTED MOON'
Introduced in 1989. A stunning colour combination, eye-catching in the garden or as a cut flower. Fragrance is only slight, but its cheerful colouring compensates. Height: 75 cm (2½ ft). Spread: 60 cm (2 ft).

'PAUL SHIRVILLE'
Introduced in 1983, and one of the best pink varieties. Plentiful blooms and a strong scent are coupled with vigorous growth and plenty of foliage. It has won many international awards. Height: 1 m (3 ft). Spread: 60 cm (2 ft).

'PEACE'
Introduced in 1945, and one of the most famous roses of all time. There are now better varieties, but it is still a beautiful rose and many grow it because it is such a familiar old favourite. Little scent. Height: 1.2 m (4 ft). Spread: 75 cm (2½ ft).

'PEAUDOUCE'
Introduced in 1985, and now established as a leading variety in its colour range. An excellent rose for cutting, but its fragrance is only slight. Height: 1 m (3 ft). Spread: 60 cm (2 ft).

'PICCADILLY'
Introduced in 1960, and highly regarded at the time, it is still a popular bicolour variety. It comes into bloom early and is free-flowering. Its drawbacks are its slight fragrance and blooms that quickly open wide and lose their shape. Height: 1 m (3 ft). Spread: 60 cm (2 ft).

'POLAR STAR'
Introduced in 1982, and Rose of the Year in 1985. The well-shaped blooms are carried on vigorous shoots, and the dark green foliage acts as a pleasing backdrop for the white flowers. It has a spicy perfume, and good weather-resistance. Height: 1 m (3 ft). Spread: 60 cm (2 ft).

'PRIMA BALLERINA'
Introduced in 1957. Well-shaped blooms with a strong and typical rose scent. Vigorous growth, but it is unfortunately susceptible to mildew and flowering is not always prolific. Height: 1 m (3 ft). Spread: 60 cm (2 ft).

'PRINCESS ROYAL'
Introduced in 1992. One of the best hybrid teas for shape and colour, and with the bonus of a pleasant spicy fragrance. Strong, bushy growth. Height: 1 m (3 ft). Spread: 60 cm (2 ft).

'ROSEMARY HARKNESS'
Introduced in 1985. A popular choice because of its fragrance, and excellent for cuttings as well as bedding. Well-branched vigorous growth makes it a reliable garden rose. Height: 1 m (3 ft). Spread: 60 cm (2 ft).

'ROYAL WILLIAM'
Introduced in 1987, in which year it was voted Rose of the Year. It is currently one of the best of its colour with a heady scent, and the sturdy bushes have strong, healthy foliage. Height: 1 m (3 ft). Spread: 60 cm (2 ft).

'RUBY WEDDING'
Introduced in 1979. Not an exceptional rose, but popular as an anniversary gift because of its name. The fragrance is only slight, but the rose makes a pleasing display in small groups in a border. Height: 1 m (3 ft). Spread: 60 cm (2 ft).

'SAVOY HOTEL'
Introduced in 1989. It has perfectly shaped blooms, is excellent as a cut flower with its strong stems and plentiful foliage, and a first-rate hybrid tea for bedding. Moderate scent. Height: 1 m (3 ft). Spread: 60 cm (2 ft).

'SILVER JUBILEE'
Introduced in 1978, and still one of the best hybrid teas for general planting. It flowers freely and the vigorous, bushy plants are very disease-resistant. It has won many awards. Light fragrance. Height: 1 m (3 ft). Spread: 60 cm (2 ft).

'SIMBA'
Introduced in 1981. One of the most perfectly formed yellow hybrid teas, it makes an excellent cut flower. Slight fragrance. The plants are bushy and it is one of the best yellows for bedding. Height: 75 cm (2½ ft). Spread: 60 cm (2 ft).

'TROIKA'
Introduced in 1971, and sometimes known as 'Royal Dane'. An excellent all-round rose, good for bedding, excellent for cuttings, and large enough to exhibit, with good weather-tolerance and disease-resistance. Height: 1 m (3 ft). Spread: 60 cm (2 ft).

'TYNWALD'
Introduced in 1979. Large flowers on sturdy stems with lush, disease-resistant foliage. Moderate fragrance. Height: 1 m (3 ft). Spread: 60 cm (2 ft).

'ANGELA RIPPON'
Introduced in 1978. A bushy, leafy plant, it makes a good choice for the edge of a border as well as raised beds and containers. Because of its height, it is classified as a patio rose in some catalogues. Height: 45 cm (1½ ft). Spread: 30 cm (1 ft).

'BABY MASQUERADE'
Introduced in 1966, and deservedly still a favourite. It grows freely and blooms continuously over a long period. It looks better planted in groups than as an individual plant. Height: 30 cm (1 ft). Spread: 23 cm (9 in).

'BUSH BABY'
Introduced in 1986. It has bushy growth with plenty of foliage, and is pleasing both as a massed group or grown as an individual plant. Height: 30 cm (1 ft). Spread: 23 cm (9 in).

'CINDERELLA'
Introduced in 1953. The white flowers tend to have a touch of pink, especially in cool weather. The bushy plants have disease-resistant foliage. Height: 30 cm (1 ft). Spread: 23 cm (9 in).

'ORANGE SUNBLAZE'
Introduced in 1981, and still widely grown for its large and long-lasting flowers. Bushy growth, and free-flowering, but unfortunately there is no scent. Height: 38 cm (15 in). Spread: 23 cm (9 in).

'RED ACE'
Introduced in 1982. Perfectly formed flowers, a strong colour, and compact growth make this a highly desirable miniature. Height: 30 cm (1 ft). Spread: 23 cm (9 in).

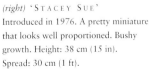

(left) 'RED SUNBLAZE'
Introduced in 1980. A vivid rose that makes a great splash of colour despite its small size. It repeat-flowers well. Height: 38 cm (15 in). Spread: 23 cm (9 in).

(right) 'STACEY SUE'
Introduced in 1976. A pretty miniature that looks well proportioned. Bushy growth. Height: 38 cm (15 in). Spread: 30 cm (1 ft).

Patio Roses

'ANNA FORD'
Introduced in 1980, and one of the
leading patio varieties, having amassed
many top international awards. A good
choice for an edging as well as a patio bed
or pot, but with little fragrance. Height:
45 cm (1½ ft). Spread: 45 cm (1½ ft).

'CONSERVATION'
Introduced in 1988. An eye-catching rose
with flowers well set off by abundant
bright, glossy foliage. Although not
strongly fragrant, it does have a pleasant
scent. Height: 45 cm (1½ ft).
Spread: 45 cm (1½ ft).

'DRUMMER BOY'
Introduced in 1987, and an outstanding
variety for brilliance of colour and
profusion of flowers. It has little scent.
Plant in small groups towards the front of
a border, or as a low edging or hedge, as
well as in containers. Height: 45 cm
(1½ft). Spread: 45 cm (1½ ft).

'GENTLE TOUCH'
Introduced in 1986, when it was voted
Rose of the Year – one of the first patio
roses to win the title. The dainty blooms
are produced in profusion, sometimes
covering the strong and sturdy plants.
Little scent. Height: 60 cm (2 ft).
Spread: 45 cm (1½ ft).

'HAKUUN'
Introduced in 1962, and still one of the
finest whites. The name means "white
cloud", which accurately describes the
appearance of the plant in full bloom.
There is only a slight fragrance. Height:
60 cm (2 ft). Spread: 45 cm (1½ ft).

'PEEK A BOO'
Introduced in 1981. Prolific in bloom, this
little rose is a good choice to fill in gaps
towards the front of a border, or to grow
in a tub. Height: 60 cm (2 ft).
Spread: 45 cm (1½ ft).

'RAY OF SUNSHINE'
Introduced in 1989. An unfading yellow,
with a backing of small, shiny foliage.
Quick to repeat-flower, but only a slight
scent. Height: 45 cm (1½ ft).
Spread: 45 cm (1½ ft).

'ROBIN REDBREAST'
Introduced in 1984. An excellent low-
growing plant that could be used instead
of summer bedding. It is spectacular
planted *en masse*, and ideal for edging a
border. Height: 45 cm (1½ ft).
Spread: 45 cm (1½ ft).

'ROSABELL'
Introduced in 1988, this is a charming
variety with flowers shaped like those of
an old rose. It flowers prolifically and
there is a slight scent. Height: 45 cm
(1½ ft). Spread: 45 cm (1½ ft).

'RUGUL'
Introduced in 1973. Grown mainly for its
bright yellow colour, which does not fade
readily in hot sun. Good repeat-flowering
is also a feature, but there is little scent. It
is sometimes listed as a miniature. Height:
45 cm (1½ ft). Spread: 45 cm (1½ ft).

'SWEET MAGIC'
Introduced in 1987, when it won the Rose
of the Year award. Beautifully formed
flowers with a light fragrance, on bushes
well clothed with foliage. Height: 45 cm
(1½ ft). Spread: 45 cm (1½ ft).

'TOP MARKS'
Introduced in 1992, when it won the
highest score ever at that time in the Rose
of the Year trials, as well as other awards
in several countries. Its strong points are a
dazzling colour and prolific blooming. It
also has good disease-resistance but is
only lightly scented. Height: 45 cm
(1½ ft). Spread: 45 cm (1½ ft).

$\mathcal{S}$HRUB ROSES

'ANDERSONII'

A *Rosa canina* hybrid, but the flowers are larger than those of the dog rose. They are sweetly scented and followed by showy red hips in autumn. Height: 2.1 m (7 ft). Spread: 2.4 m (8 ft).

'BELLE DE CRÉCY'

A gallica rose bred before 1829, with quartered-rosette, sweetly scented flowers, produced in abundance in mid-summer. It is considered to be one of the best gallicas, but has a laxer habit than most and may require some support. Height: 1.2 m (4 ft). Spread: 1 m (3 ft).

'BLAIRII NUMBER TWO'

A Bourbon rose raised in 1845. Untrained it will grow into an arching shrub, but its vigour makes it suitable for growing on a pyramid or pergola or against a wall, and it is often catalogued as a climber. The sweetly scented flowers are produced mainly in mid-summer. Height against a wall: 4.5 m (15 ft). Spread: 2.4 m (8 ft).

'BUFF BEAUTY'

A hybrid musk, sometimes classified as a modern shrub rose, probably bred before 1939. The sweetly scented flowers are carried in two flushes, the autumn flower-ing being less profuse. Mildew may be a problem in late summer. Height: 1.5 m (5 ft). Spread: 1.5 m (5 ft).

'CÉCILE BRUNNER'

A polyantha rose sometimes classified as a China rose, introduced in 1881. It produces its delicately scented flowers from summer to autumn. It used also to be known as 'The Sweetheart Rose'. A climbing form is often planted. Height: 1 m (3 ft). Spread: 1 m (3 ft).

'CÉLESTE'

An alba rose whose date of introduction is uncertain, though it is certainly very old. The flowers are sweetly scented and carried on lax, spreading stems. There is a bonus of red hips in autumn. It is sometimes called 'Celestial'. Height: 1.8 m (6 ft). Spread: 1.8 m (6 ft).

'CHAPEAU DE NAPOLÉON'

A centifolia rose bred in the 1820s and now more correctly known as *Rosa x centifolia* 'Cristata'. Its richly scented flowers open flat and are sometimes quartered. The name 'Chapeau de Napoléon' refers to the heavily mossed buds which look like tricorn hats. Height: 1.5 m (5 ft). Spread: 1.2 m (4 ft).

'CHARLES DE MILLS'

A gallica rose of unknown parentage and date of introduction. It makes a compact shrub with moderately scented crimson flowers, which fade into purple and grey tones as they mature. The stems are slender and may require staking. Height: 1.2 m (4 ft). Spread: 1 m (3 ft).

'COMPLICATA'

A gallica rose of uncertain origin, and untypical of most gallicas. The single flowers are sweetly scented and produced in abundance in summer. The leaves are matt greyish-green. It can be used as a rambler among other shrubs in a wild garden or trained on a pillar. Height: 2.4 m (8 ft). Spread: 2.4 m (8 ft).

'CONSTANCE SPRY'

A modern shrub rose, sometimes classified as an 'English' rose, introduced in 1961. The peony-like flowers are heavily scented, but it flowers only once in summer. Untrained, it makes a lax shrub, but it can be grown as a climber on a pillar. Height: 1.8 m (6 ft). Spread: 1.8 m (6 ft).

'FÉLICITÉ PARMENTIER'

An alba rose, known since about 1834, that grows as a compact shrub. Its highly scented flowers are borne in mid-summer, the densely packed petals fading almost to white in hot sun and reflexing to form a ball-shape. It is one of the daintiest albas, suitable for a small garden. Height: 1.2 m (4 ft). Spread: 1.2 m (4 ft).

'GRAHAM THOMAS'

A modern shrub or 'English' rose, raised in 1983. The pleasantly scented flowers are produced in succession from summer to autumn. Named in honour of the great English rosarian Graham Stuart Thomas. Height: 1.2 m (4 ft). Spread: 1.2 m (4 ft).

'GRUSS AN AACHEN'

A polyantha rose sometimes classified as a modern rose or as a cluster-flowered bush, bred around 1909. The flowers are delicately scented and carried in clusters from summer to autumn. Its long flowering season and low growth habit make it an outstanding rose. Height: 1 m (3 ft). Spread: 1 m (3 ft).

'ISPAHAN'

A damask rose first recorded in 1832 but probably much older; it may be Persian in origin. The flowers are richly scented, but there is only the one flush in summer. However, it has a longer flowering period than most other damasks and is in bloom for up to six weeks. Height: 1.5 m (5 ft). Spread: 1.2 m (4 ft).

'KÖNIGIN VON DÄNEMARK'

An alba rose, produced in 1826, that makes an elegant bush with richly scented flowers in summer. It has a long flowering season – up to six weeks – and the blooms have good resistance to wet weather. The variety is sometimes sold as 'Queen of Denmark'. Height: 1.5 m (5 ft). Spread: 1.2 m (4 ft).

'L. D. BRAITHWAITE'

A modern shrub rose introduced in 1988, and one of the best for continuity of flower, with top quality blooms and a rich fragrance. Height: 1.2 m (4 ft). Spread: 1.2 m (4 ft).

'MADAME HARDY'

A damask rose dating from 1832. The strongly scented flowers are borne in profusion in summer. This is generally considered to be one of the most sumptuous of old roses, though the flowers may be spoilt by rain. Height: 1.5 m (5 ft). Spread: 1.5 m (5 ft).

ROSA 'ALBA MAXIMA'

An alba rose dating from at least the 15th century. The somewhat untidy flowers are very fragrant, and followed by red hips. It is otherwise known as the 'Great Double White', 'Jacobite' or 'Cheshire Rose', while some consider it to be the 'White Rose of York'. Height: 1.8 m (6 ft). Spread: 1.5 m (5 ft).

ROSA RUGOSA

A species rose with distinctive wrinkled leaves and bright pink single flowers, followed in autumn by very large rounded hips. It is a good choice for a rose hedge, especially in coastal areas. Height: 1.8 m (6 ft). Spread: 1.5 m (5 ft).

ROSA XANTHINA 'CANARY BIRD'

A form of wild rose of uncertain origin but assumed to have been introduced after 1907. It flowers early, in late spring, and though the flowers are single they are large and conspicuous, with fern-like leaves as a foil. It is sometimes available as a standard. Height: 2.1 m (7 ft). Spread: 2.1 m (7 ft).

'ROSERAIE DE L'HAŸ'

A rugosa hybrid introduced in 1901. The heavily scented flowers are borne continuously through summer and into autumn. The bright green leaves are heavily crinkled. This weather-resistant rose makes an excellent hedge. Height: 2.1 m (7 ft). Spread: 2.1 m (7 ft).

'STANWELL PERPETUAL'

A Scotch rose, raised in 1838, with sweetly scented flowers produced almost continuously throughout the summer. The leaves are grey-green. It makes a good hedge. Height: 1.5 m (5 ft). Spread: 1.5 m (5 ft).

'WILLIAM LOBB'

A moss rose introduced in 1855, with highly scented flowers that open from heavily "mossed" buds. This is a vigorous rose that makes a sprawling upright shrub. It can be trained as a short climber on a pillar or against a wall. Height: 1.8 m (6 ft). Spread: 1.8 m (6 ft).

DECORATING WITH ROSES

Roses are incredibly versatile and can be used to decorate your home in a variety of ways from table arrangements and baskets to garlands and swags. The following pages will help you to create beautiful displays that will enhance any room in the house.

CARE AND CONDITIONING OF CUT ROSES

Whether you are buying roses or cutting them from the garden, always choose those in the very best condition. Reputable florists, supermarkets and flower stalls take pride in their flowers, selling only good-quality blooms and having the knowledge and experience to keep them that way.

If you are cutting roses from the garden, it is best to do this first thing in the morning, when their water content is highest. Cut the flowers at a sharp angle just above a leaf node and be sure not to be so greedy that you rob each bush of all its blooms or destroy its overall appearance! Place the flowers immediately in a bucket of water, where they can have a long drink before you arrange them.

If you are buying roses, make sure they are well wrapped to avoid excess evaporation and to protect their delicate petals. For long journeys it is better to put them in a bucket of water but, if this is impractical, ask the retailer to cover the stem ends with damp paper. As soon as you reach home, give the flowers a long drink in deep tepid water.

Before arranging the flowers, always cut off any foliage that will fall below the water line in the container or vase. Make a long, diagonal cut from the bottom of each stem, as this will provide the maximum area for water intake. Rose stems should never be crushed with a hammer as so many books advocate. Independent research has proved that this method

ABOVE: As a gift, lay a bunch of roses and foliage diagonally on a square of paper and fold around the stems. Tie securely with raffia or ribbon.

destroys the delicate plant cells and makes the stalk less efficient in taking up water; it also encourages the spread of bacterial infection.

Bacteria block the stems and cause the drooping heads so often experienced with shop-bought roses. You can avoid this problem by always using scrupulously clean vases, removing all leaves below the water level and adding commercially formulated flower food. This simple powder contains the correct amount of a mild and completely harmless disinfectant, which inhibits bacterial growth, together with a sugar that

feeds the roses and encourages the flowers to mature and open. If flower food is added to the water it is unnecessary to change it, but it may need topping up in warm weather. Although many people have their own recipes for increasing roses' longevity – lemonade, aspirins, household bleach and so on – flower food is by far the most successful way of keeping roses at their best for longer.

For arrangements using plastic foam, make holes for the rose and other stems with a wooden skewer. If you push the rose stem straight into the foam, particles of foam may become lodged in the base of the stem and prevent good water uptake, causing premature wilting.

If rose heads have wilted, and this may be a result of bacterial infection or an airlock somewhere in the stem, it may be possible to revive them by wrapping them in strong paper and standing the stems in tepid water up to their heads for several hours after first cutting at least 5 cm (2 in) from the end of each stem. If this treatment fails, even more drastic action will be needed and the roses will have to be cut very short in order to perk up their drooping heads.

Finally, there are many theories about rose thorns. Again, research has proved that bacteria may invade the gashes left in the stem when thorns are cut off, so it is better to do this only if the roses are being carried in a bouquet or posy where thorns could prick the hands.

1 Always place roses in a bucket of tepid water for a couple of hours after purchase or cutting.

4 If thorns have to be removed because the roses are being used in a bouquet, use sharp scissors to cut them off, but not too close to the stem.

2 After choosing the vase, cut off any leaves that will fall below the water level, as these will rot and stagnate the water.

5 Add a proprietary flower food to the water in the vase to prolong the life of cut flowers and help to keep the vase water clear.

7 Give first aid to wilting flower heads by wrapping them securely in stiff paper and standing them in a large container of tepid water for a few hours.

3 Using a very sharp knife or pair of scissors, cut the stem diagonally to ensure maximum water uptake.

6 It is sometimes possible to revive wilted roses by cutting the stems very short.

DRYING AND STEAMING ROSES

DRYING ROSES

Roses have been dried for as long as they have been cultivated; their petals have been used in potpourri or the whole stems in decorative arrangements when the fresh flowers were scarce. The Elizabethans preserved roses by immersing them completely in dry sand and keeping them warm until all the moisture had been drawn out. In Victorian times, when houses were heated with open coal fires, which shortened the lives of fresh blooms, intricate dried arrangements were painstakingly created and then covered in glass domes to keep them

dust-free. These rather tortured, contrived designs have long since lost their appeal in preference for looser, more natural arrangements and contemporary designs using dried flowers have gained a new popularity.

There are three principal ways of drying roses: in the air, in a microwave oven and using a desiccant. The latest commercial method is freeze-drying. This successful technique was originally developed as a means to store penicillin and blood plasma during the Second World War. It requires specialized freezers so it is no use putting a bunch of roses in a domestic model. The process can

take up to two weeks and is therefore very expensive but the results are stunning, producing dried roses with all their former intensity of colour and, in some cases, even preserving their perfume. Flowers or bouquets dried by this method can allegedly last for about five years before they start to fade or disintegrate.

Air-drying is the most common method and by far the cheapest as it requires no more than the cost of the roses. This method is best for rosebuds that are just about to open but

BELOW: The easiest way to dry roses is to hang them upside-down in a dark, warm and well ventilated room.

ABOVE: Once the roses are completely dry, carefully strip off the leaves and tie the buds tightly together. Combined with a halo of dried lavender, a small posy in a terracotta pot makes a delightful gift.

DESICCANT-DRYING

Desiccant-drying using silica gel crystals or fine sand may be used for fully open roses.

Silica gel is available from some larger pharmacies.

1 Put 1 cm (½ in) of the crystals or sand in an airtight container and lay the rose-heads face up.

2 Cover very carefully with more sifted desiccant until every part of the flower is concealed. Then tightly seal the container and keep at room temperature for approximately seven to ten days before removing from the desiccant.

still have their bud shape. They need to be hung somewhere warm, dry and dark with good ventilation for a couple of weeks – a large airing-cupboard may be ideal. Stringing them together washing-line-style speeds up the process and prevents any moisture being trapped between the flowers, which may develop into mildew. Once they are completely dry, handle them with care as the stems are very brittle. A tight bunch of rose-buds packed together in a small terracotta pot will give added impact to the now-faded colour of the petals. A gentle blow on the lowest setting of a hair drier usually removes most of any dust.

As the flowers need to fit the radius of the turntable, microwave-drying is suitable only for arrange-ments requiring quite short stems. Lay the flowers on greaseproof paper and put into the microwave oven on the lowest setting. The roses need to be checked every minute to prevent "over-cooking".

STEAMING ROSES

This simple technique can greatly improve the appearance of dried roses which are imported in large boxes with up to 25 bunches per box. Frequently, some or all of the bunches arrive at their destination rather squashed. This process will give them a new lease of life, but take care. Never try to open the very centre of the rose, which is often discoloured. The process also works very well for peonies.

1 Bring a kettle to the boil. Hold the rose by its stem, head down-wards, in the steam for a few seconds, until the outside petals start to waver.

2 Remove the rose from the steam and gently push back the outer petals, one by one. Do not tug at the petals or you will find them coming away in your hand.

3 If necessary, repeat the steaming process and continue to open the petals, working from the outside towards the centre.

EQUIPMENT AND CONTAINERS

EQUIPMENT

Cellophane · This is useful as a wrapping for a bouquet, as a waterproof lining for containers and scrunched up in a vase of water to support flower stems.

Florist's Adhesive · This sticky glue can be used to attach synthetic and delicate materials which would not withstand the heat of a glue gun.

Florist's Adhesive Tape · This tape is used to secure foam in containers.

Plastic Foam · Plastic foam comes in a vast range of shapes, sizes and densities, and is available for dry and fresh flowers. Do not re-soak foam used for fresh flowers once it has dried out.

Florist's Scissors · You need a strong, sharp pair of scissors which must be sturdy enough to cut woody stems and even wires.

Florist's Tape · This tape is not adhesive, but the heat of your hands will help secure it to itself. The tape is used to conceal wires and seal stem ends to give an attractive finish.

Florist's Wire · Wire is used to support, control and secure materials, and to extend, strengthen or replace stems. It is available in pre-cut lengths or on a reel. Always use the lightest gauge of wire you can. One of the most useful gauges when working with roses is .71mm (22g).

Glue Gun · The glue gun is electrically powered and fed by sticks of glue, which it melts. It is invaluable in allowing the arranger to attach dried or fresh materials to swags, garlands or circlets securely, cleanly and efficiently. Take care at all times when using a glue gun. Never leave a hot glue gun unattended and avoid using on delicate materials.

Paper Ribbon · This comes in a large range of soft colours. Cut the length required in its twisted state and carefully untwist and flatten it before creating your bows.

Raffia · A natural alternative to string and ribbon, raffia can be used to tie a hand-arranged, spiralled bunch, or to attach bunches to garlands and swags.

Rose Stripper · Squeeze the metal claws together and pull the stripper along the stem to remove thorns and leaves. There is also a blade attachment, to cut stem ends at an angle.

Satin Ribbon · Satin is preferable to synthetic because it is so much softer.

Secateurs · These are necessary to cut the tougher, thicker stems.

String · String is essential when tying spiralled bunches, making garlands or attaching foliage to gates and posts.

Wire Mesh · Plastic foam offers more flexibility but wire mesh is useful. In creating large displays, wire mesh strengthens the foam and prevents it from crumbling. The mesh should be laid over the top of the foam, wrapped around the sides and wedged between it and the container, then secured in place with florist's adhesive tape.

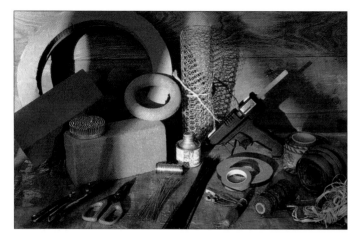

LEFT: Start with the basic equipment and add items as your skill develops.

CONTAINERS

While an enormous range of suitable, practical, purpose-made containers is available to the flower arranger, with a little imagination alternatives will present themselves. An old jug or teapot, a pretty mug, an unusual tin, a jam jar, all offer the arranger interesting opportunities.

For fresh flowers, the container must be watertight or properly lined. Consider the scale and proportion of the container both to the particular flowers you are going to use, and the type of arrangement.

Do not forget the container can be a hidden part of the design, simply there to hold the arrangement, or it can be an integral and important feature in the overall finished arrangement.

Baking Tins · Apart from the usual shapes, star, heart, club, spade and diamond shaped baking tins can be used very effectively.

They are particularly good for massed designs, either of fresh or dried flowers, but remember, the tin may need lining. ·

Baskets · Baskets are an obvious choice for country-style displays. However, there is a wide range of designs to suit many different styles.

Wire or metal baskets are ornate alternatives to wicker and twig, and have a more modern look. Most baskets will need a waterproof lining.

Cast-iron Urns · Though expensive and heavy, cast-iron urns are attractive and will underpin either a large and flowing or contemporary and linear arrangement.

ABOVE: *A varied selection from the vast range of containers that can be used for flower arranging.*

Enamelled Containers · Containers in strong primary colours work well with similarly brightly coloured flowers to produce vibrant displays.

Galvanized Metal Buckets and Pots · These will not rust and their texture is ideal for contemporary displays of both fresh and dried flowers. Lots of shapes and sizes are available but even an old-fashioned bucket can be used.

Glass Vases · The obvious choice, in a wide range; clear glass allows the arrangement to speak for itself. Keep the water scrupulously clean. Frosted, coloured, textured and cut glass all have their place.

Pitchers · Pitchers are ideal receptacles, whether ceramic, glass, enamelled or galvanized metal; short, tall, thin or fat. Displays can range from the rustic and informal to the grand and extravagant.

Pre-formed Plastic Foam Shapes · Pre-formed plastic foam comes in a wide range of shapes and sizes and "novelty" designs, each with a watertight backing. Equivalent foam shapes are available for dried flowers.

Terracotta Pots · If the arrangement is built in plastic foam, line the pot with cellophane first. Alternatively just pop a jam jar or bowl into the pot to hold the water.

Terracotta pots can be changed very effectively by rubbing them with coloured chalks, or treating them with gold leaf. Organic materials, such as sour milk, will encourage a surface growth to develop, to "age" pots.

Wooden Trugs and Boxes · Particularly suitable for enhancing country-style designs, rubbing with coloured chalk can create an entirely new look. Remember to line with waterproof material.

Techniques

Taping stems and wires

Stems and wires are covered with florist's tape for three reasons. First, cut materials which have been wired can no longer take up water and covering these with tape seals in the moisture that already exists in the stem. Second, the tape conceals the wires. Third, wired dried materials are covered with florist's tape to ensure that the material does not slip out of the wired mount.

1 Hold the wired stem near its top with the end of a length of florist's tape between the thumb and index finger of your left hand (or the opposite way if you are left-handed). Hold the remainder of the length of tape at 45° to the wired stem, keeping it taut. Starting at the top of the stem, just above the wires, rotate the flower slowly, to wrap the tape around both the stem and wires, working down.

2 While taping the wired stem you may wish to add further stems, setting the flower-heads at different heights as you tape, to create "units". Finally, fasten off just above the end of the wires, by squeezing the tape against itself to stick it securely.

Making a stay wire

1 Group together four florist's wires, each overlapping the next by about 3 cm (1¼ in). Start taping the wires together from one end.

2 As the tape reaches the end of the first wire add another wire to the remaining three ends of wires and continue taping, and so on, adding wires and taping four together until you achieve the required length.

Single leg mount

This is for wiring flowers which have a strong natural stem or where a double weight of wire is not necessary.

1 Hold the flowers or foliage between your thumb and index finger, while taking the weight of the material across the top of your hand. Position a wire behind the stem one-third up from the bottom.

2 Bend the wire ends together with one leg shorter than the other. Holding the short wire leg parallel with the stem, wrap the long wire leg around both the stem and the other wire leg. Straighten the long wire.

Double-leg mount

This is formed in the same way as the single-leg mount but extends the stem with two equal-length wire legs.

1 Hold the flower or foliage between the thumb and index finger of your left hand (or opposite way if you are left-handed) while taking the weight of the plant material across the top of your hand. Position a wire of appropriate weight and length behind the stem about one-third of the way up from the bottom. One-third of the wire should be to one side of the stem with two-thirds to the other. Bend the wire parallel to the stem. One leg will be about twice as long as the other.

Holding the shorter leg against the stem, wrap the longer leg around both stem and the other wire to secure. Straighten both legs which should now be of equal length.

WIRING A ROSE-HEAD

Roses have relatively thick, woody stems so, to make them suitable for use in intricate work the natural stem needs to be replaced with a wire stem.

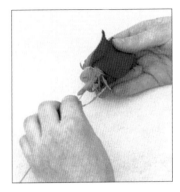

1 Cut the stem of the rose to a length of about 3 cm (1¼ in). Push one end of a florist's wire through the seed-box of the rose at the side. Holding the head of the rose in your left hand (opposite way if you are left-handed), wrap the wire firmly around and down the stem.

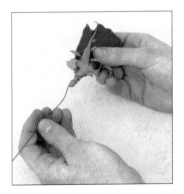

2 Straighten the remaining wire to extend the natural stem. Cover the wire and stem with florist's tape.

TYING POSIES

Simple, hand-tied posies are a very special gift and their diminutive size implies an intimacy that makes them personal and unique. The smaller the posy, the tinier and more delicate the flowers and foliage need to be. Wispy, frond-like leaves define the shape of individual flower-heads, particularly if the colours are similar, and this will give the posy more clarity.

1 Put the roses in a spiralling bunch and surround with rose leaves. Bind the flowers with raffia and trim the stems. Leaving enough ribbon to tie a bow, start winding the ribbon from the top, overlapping each twist to conceal the raffia and the stems.

2 When you reach the bottom, tuck the ribbon over the base of the stems and then wind the ribbon back up the stems.

3 When you reach the starting point, tie the ribbon in a knot before adding a bow and cut the ribbon ends on a slant to help to prevent any fraying.

$\mathcal{F}$RESH VALENTINE TERRACOTTA POTS

2 Build a dome-shaped foliage outline in proportion to each pot, using ming fern in the larger pot and ivy leaves in the smaller one.

3 In the larger pot, arrange 'Santini' chrysanthemums amongst the ming fern. In the small pot, distribute the phlox amongst the ivy.

$\mathcal{W}$ith luck, Valentine's Day brings with it red roses, but these small jewel-like arrangements present them in an altogether different way. The deep red of the roses visually links the two pots: contrasting with the acid lime green of 'Santini' chrysanthemums in one, and combining richly with purple phlox in the other.

MATERIALS
half block plastic foam
2 small terracotta pots, 1 slightly
  larger than the other
cellophane
knife
scissors
ming fern
ivy leaves

5 stems 'Santini' spray
  chrysanthemums
6 stems purple phlox
18 stems dark red roses

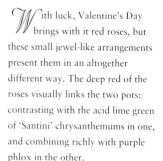

1 Soak the plastic foam in water. Line both the terracotta pots with cellophane. Cut the foam into small blocks and wedge them into the lined pots. Trim the cellophane to fit. Do not trim too close to the edge of the pot.

4 Strip the leaves and thorns from the roses, cut the stems to length and arrange in both displays.

ABOVE LEFT: *Arrange together or on their own.*

Small Fresh Rose Valentine's Ring

2 Make hairpin shapes out of the florist's wires and pin small pieces of bun moss on to the foam ring between the ivy leaves. Do this throughout the foliage but to a thinner density than the ivy.

3 Cut the leaves and thorns off the roses. Cut the rose stems to approximately 3.5 cm (1⅜ in) long and push them into the foam until the ring is evenly covered. The ivy leaves should still be visible in between the rose-heads.

While this delightful floral circlet could be used at any time of the year, the impact created by the massed red roses makes it particularly appropriate to Valentine's Day. It can be hung on a wall or, with a candle at its centre, used as a table decoration for a romantic dinner for two.

MATERIALS
15 cm (6 in) diameter plastic foam
   ring
dark green ivy leaves
florist's wires
bun moss
20 stems dark red roses
scissors

1 Soak the plastic foam ring in water. Push individual, medium-sized ivy leaves into the foam, to create an even foliage outline all around the ring.

ABOVE LEFT: If you receive a Valentine's Day bouquet of red roses, why not recycle them? After the rose blooms have fully blown open, cut down their stems for use in this circlet, to extend their lives.

ROSE CROWNS FOR ALL SEASONS

Roses can be enjoyed all year round. Garden roses start blooming in mid-spring and continue into late autumn, if the weather is mild. During the barren winter months, there are still hundreds of commercially grown roses to choose from. Just as a garden enjoys a change of season with different colours, shapes and scents, you can acknowledge the shifting calendar inside your home. It is a practical investment to acquire a versatile container – perhaps an old china soup tureen or vase – that gives scope to a range of decorative ideas. It should be large enough to hold several small vases and candles, and also be deep enough to be used as a planter.

SPRING

The darker pink and red freesias used in this arrangement have a strong scent. Paler pink tulips present a contrast in shape to the 'Louise Odier' rose, a camellia-like Bourbon rose which flowers almost continuously through the summer. The lacy foliage of bupleurum has the same delicate qualities as *Alchemilla mollis*, another good filler for later in the year.

SUMMER

Sunflowers radiate bright vitality and are synonymous with hot summer days. The smaller-headed varieties are more practical for arrangements, as those with heads the size of dinner plates are too heavy and dominating and are best left to grow in the

SPRING

SUMMER

*A*UTUMN

garden. 'Tina' is one of the commercially grown larger-flowered spray roses; it has a rich buttery colour and a slight scent.

AUTUMN

Rosa pimpinellifolia or 'Scotch Briar' is an ancient hardy rose which produces creamy-white single flowers and, later, almost black hips. The latter are combined here with dusty pink mop-heads of hydrangea and a stunning commercially grown rose called 'Baccarole'. Its red wine-coloured petals develop a faint but obvious perfume.

WINTER

Create an elegant centrepiece for a Christmas table with white and cream roses, varying shades of green foliage and non-drip candles. Several very late flowering 'Boule de Neige' Bourbon roses are supplemented with the commercially grown 'White Success'. Grey-green eucalyptus blends with symphoricarpos (snowberry) and trailing variegated ivy.

*W*INTER

ABOVE: A crown-shaped container is packed with an assortment of different shapes and sizes of jars and bottles.

WARNING: Never leave candles burning unattended.

OLD-FASHIONED GARDEN ROSE ARRANGEMENT

LEFT: *The technique is to mass several varieties of rose, whose papery petals will achieve a textural mix of colour and scent.*

2 Position the longer-stemmed blooms in the pitcher with the heads massed tightly together. This ensures that the cut stems are supported and so can simply be placed directly in the water.

The beautiful full-blown blooms of these antique-looking roses give an opulent and romantic feel to a very simple combination of flower and container. This arrangement deserves centre stage in any room setting.

MATERIALS

watertight container, to put inside plant pot
squat weathered terracotta pot
pitcher
short- and long-stemmed garden roses
scissors

1 Place the watertight container inside the terracotta pot and fill with water. Fill the pitcher as well. Select and prepare your blooms and remove the lower foliage and thorns.

3 Mass shorter, more open flower-heads in the container inside the plant pot with the stems hidden and the heads showing just above the rim of the pot. The heads look best if kept either all on one level or in a slight dome shape. If fewer flowers are used, wire mesh or plastic foam may be needed to control the positions of individual blooms.

RUBY WEDDING DISPLAY

Formal looking, but simple in construction, this Ruby Wedding arrangement is a lavish mass of deep purple tulips and velvety red roses set against the dark glossy green of camellia leaves. A beautiful paper bow completes the effect.

MATERIALS
bowl
10 short stems camellia foliage
scissors
20 red roses
10 purple tulips
paper ribbon

ABOVE: Designed as a table arrangement complete with celebratory bow around its container, this display of rich and passionate colours would be a magnificent gift.

1 Approximately three-quarters fill the bowl with water. Remove the lower foliage from the camellia stems and roses and remove the thorns. Cut the stems of camellia and roses to 7.5 cm (3 in) longer than the depth of the container. Arrange the camellia stems in the bowl, to create a low domed foliage outline, within which the flowers will be arranged. Arrange half the roses evenly throughout the camellia foliage.

2 Cut the tulip stems to approximately 7.5 cm (3 in) longer than the depth of the bowl and strip away any remaining lower leaves from the stems. Position the tulips in the display, distributing them evenly throughout the roses and camellia. Finally, add the remaining roses evenly throughout the arrangement to complete a dense, massed flower effect of deep red hues.

3 Form a festive bow from the paper ribbon. The bow should be substantial but it is important that it is kept in scale with the display. To complete the arrangement, tie the bow to the container so that it sits on the front.

TABLE STYLING WITH ROSES

Even the simplest meal can be transformed into something quite special with the addition of a few beautiful flowers to the table. In summer, when garden roses are plentiful, it takes only a few to add their delicious, delicate scent to a table setting. The strongest perfume comes from those that are in full bloom. Their heavy heads need to be cut short and may need the support of some other foliage, such as lavender or rosemary in a simple arrangement.

Commercially grown roses are usually sold in bud, so buy them a few days before they are needed to ensure that the roses open to produce large clusters of small flower-heads that are perfect for low arrangements. Floral designs for tables are best kept short, so diners can see across the table and plates can be passed with-out any obstacles. Alternatively, tall candelabra can be decorated with delicate foliage, with rose-heads wired to the candle holders. A piece of plastic foam fitted around the base of each candle can be concealed with foliage and short stems of roses gently pushed into it.

For special parties, a rose tucked inside a napkin ring for each guest is a personal welcome. Co-ordinating the colour of the flowers with the food and table linen looks stylish and professional. A table centre of floating candles and roses is a simple idea for dinner parties and can be particularly attractive if both roses and candles

ABOVE: 'Felicia' is one of the finest of the hybrid musk roses and three or four blooms arranged with a few sprigs of rosemary in a small glass inside a terracotta pot make a natural tablesetting. Commercially grown 'Baccarole' roses take several days to open fully and their blue-crimson colour needs only a few campanula leaves to create a rich, luxurious decoration for the table.

are sweetly scented. According to the Ancient Romans, the addition of some fragrant rose petals to the wine delayed the intoxication of its drinkers! A bottle of sparkling white or rosé wine decanted into a large glass jug and then sprinkled with petals makes a delightful way of serving this drink – or follow the recipe for Rose Petal Punch.

OPPOSITE: 'Brown Velvet' is a modern cluster-flowered rose. Just a couple of stems are needed to fill a small vase, and its dark brown-red colour makes an ideal accompaniment to a plate of strawberries.

ROSES IN DIFFERENT CONTAINERS

Virtually anything can be used to hold roses, from a simple jam jar to the most expensive crystal vase. What is more important is its shape – do avoid those types of vases with tight little necks that can take only a few stems, forcing them into an uncomfortable position. Allow the roses to be the centre of attention and increase their longevity by following the instructions for conditioning roses earlier in the book.

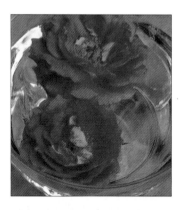

ABOVE LEFT: A shallow glass bowl holding a couple of floating rose-heads makes an effective small decoration for a bedside table or similar surface that is viewed from above. Shown here is the sweetly fragrant garden rose 'Iris Webb'.

ABOVE: A few stems of roses make a stronger statement when held together with a piece of garden raffia. This rose is the commercially grown 'Prelude' with eucalyptus stems.

LEFT: If you regularly cut roses from the garden, a wide, shallow glass dish on a pedestal is a good choice for the irregularly shaped stems, particularly of old roses. Here is the garden rose 'Felicia'.

ABOVE: *The price of commercially grown roses is often determined by the stem length. Their elegant straight stalks may be more than 60 cm (24 in) long. This beautiful rose is commercially grown 'Konfetti'.*

BELOW: *Increase the impact of the blooms by grouping them in tumblers of contrasting colours. The roses, left to right, are: 'Julia's Rose', 'Edith Holden', 'Iced Ginger', 'Peppermint Ice'; front: 'Josephine Bruce'.*

ABOVE: *A few sprays of a fragrant rose are all that are needed to impart scent to a small room or hallway. The picture shows the garden rose 'Amber Queen'. Cut roses from a bush carefully, so as not to destroy the overall shape or strip it bare, choosing blooms that would otherwise be concealed from view.*

$\mathcal{T}$IED POSY

$\mathcal{F}$lowers are at their most appealing when kept simple. Just gather together some garden cuttings and arrange them in a pretty posy that the recipient can simply unwrap and put straight into a vase, without further ado.

MATERIALS
secateurs
3 stems roses
10-12 stems eucalyptus
3 stems scabious
brown paper
ribbon

ABOVE: *"Cottage-garden" flowers, such as roses and scabious, are elegantly set against the cool green eucalyptus in this deceptively simple posy that has masses of impact.*

1 Using sharp secateurs, carefully cut each flower stem to approximately 15 cm (6 in) long. Remove the lower leaves and trim any thorns from the roses.

2 Gather the flowers together, surrounding each rose with some feathery eucalyptus, and then adding the scabious.

3 Wrap the posy with paper and secure it with a length of ribbon, tied simply in a pretty bow.

Summer Gift Basket

Fresh roses are always a welcome gift – make them into something extra special by laying them in a basket with prettily packaged, home-made strawberry jam.

MATERIALS
jar of strawberry jam
pink paper
glue
paper strawberry print
scissors
glazed pink paper
raffia
wooden basket
coloured paper
roses

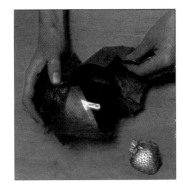

1 Make up a pretty presentation for the strawberry jam by wrapping the jar with pink paper and gluing on a paper strawberry print, to fix the paper.

2 Make a top of glazed pink paper and a raffia tie. Line the basket with coloured paper and fill it with a bunch of roses, tied with raffia, and the strawberry jam.

ABOVE: *Combining a gift of roses and home-made jam in a pretty wooden basket, with toning colours of flowers, paper and jam, makes the gift seem much more special than just giving them separately.*

MOTHER'S DAY BASKET

What could be a more delightful surprise for a mother on her special day than a basket of roses and lilies, arranged with style and sent with love? The basket, painted to tone with the flowers, becomes a permanent keepsake. It would be ideal to hold wools, sewing materials, or bath preparations.

MATERIALS

shallow basket with handle
block plastic foam
waterproof liner, such as plastic box
narrow florist's adhesive tape
scissors
long-lasting foliage, such as
    eucalyptus
several stems flowering shrub
about 12 stems pink and cream roses
about 12 stems alstroemeria
    (Peruvian lilies)
secateurs
paper ribbon
florist's wire

1 As the basket is so much part of the gift, choose a decorative one with care. The basket illustrated, with woven, twisted cane, was painted in uneven stripes of pink gloss paint, to add a touch of sparkle to the overall arrangement. This colour is repeated in the floral-printed paper ribbon bow, a flamboyant finishing touch to the design.

2 Soak the plastic foam well. Put the liner in the basket and place the block of foam in it. Cut two strips of adhesive tape and criss-cross them over the foam and down on to the sides of the basket, to hold the foam firmly in place. Arrange the tallest stems of foliage to make a fan shape at the back of the basket. Cut progressively shorter stems for the centre and front, positioning them so they droop and trail over the rim of the basket.

3 Trim the roses and remove the lower leaves and any thorns. Arrange the roses to make a gently rounded shape, alternating the colours, pink and cream, so that each complements the other.

4 Add the alstroemeria, cutting some individual flowers on short stems and positioning them close against the foam. Fill in the gaps with short sprays of flowering shrub.

5 Unfurl the twisted ribbon by pulling it out from one end.

6 Cut the length of ribbon required and tie it into a bow. Trim the ribbon ends. Thread the florist's wire through the back of the knot, twist and insert the two ends into the foam at the front of the basket. Mist the flowers with cool water, and keep the foam moist before you deliver it.

OPPOSITE: A basket arrangement is a wonderful way to give expensive roses maximum impact.

A DOZEN ROSES

The romantic tradition of giving a dozen red roses is all too often confined to Valentine's Day, when worldwide demand for red roses is so great that they become outrageously expensive. However, since roses are available all year round, why not use the idea of styling with a dozen roses for other times of the year?

Commercial rose breeders have at last recognized the universal desire for perfumed flowers and are producing exceptional roses that are scented. 'Prelude' is a beautiful dark lilac-coloured rose that has a soft sweet perfume which increases as the blooms open and can last for more than ten days.

ABOVE: *Combine the roses with complementary flowers such as darker pink arum lilies and lilac pink alstroemeria (Peruvian lilies).*

TOP: *Cut the roses quite short and arrange in a bowl filled with a close-fitting piece of well-soaked florist's foam. Add pieces of foliage to create a rounded shape.*

LEFT: *Cut the roses to different lengths and mix with other materials in different containers.*

1 Arrange the long-stemmed roses simply in a tall glass vase.

2 Buy or pick fresh green foliage to increase the size of your arrangement.

3 Using a rustic twig circle, tie small pieces of well-soaked florist's foam at intervals and cover them with foliage or moss. Carefully make small holes with a sharp stick in each piece. Place the roses in groups of two or three and keep the foam moist.

4 Make a table centrepiece of the roses in a basket with candles.

5 Line a large basket with polythene (plastic) and fill with small compatible houseplants, leaving space for one or more vases to hold the roses. Cover the surface with moss, to conceal the tops of the vases.

6 Before the roses open, hang them upside-down to air-dry.

7 Once the roses have opened but before they start to "blow", place them in a large shallow container of sand and allow to dry.

RIGHT: Tie the roses into a pompom shape, using a piece of string or garden raffia, and place in a narrow glass vase or jam jar that is tall enough to support them. Stand this in a flower pot or planter and cover the top with moss, to create the effect of a tree. Keep well topped up with water.

TABLE ARRANGEMENT WITH FRUIT AND FLOWERS

The addition of fruit brings a visual opulence to this arrangement of flowers. The sumptuous reds and purples of the figs and grapes used in this display harmonize beautifully with the rich, deep hues of the flowers. The natural bloom on the fruit combines with the velvet softness of the roses to create a textural feast for the eye. The overall effect is one of ravishing lusciousness.

MATERIALS
basket
cellophane
2 blocks plastic foam
scissors
florist's adhesive tape
1 bundle tree ivy
3 bunches red grapes
florist's wires
6 black figs
15 stems antirrhinum
15 stems amaranthus (straight, not trailing)
15 stems astilbe
20 stems red roses
5 stems hydrangea

ABOVE: *Make sure that all your chosen material enhances the colour of the roses.*

1 Line the basket with cellophane and tightly wedge in the blocks of water-soaked plastic foam. Trim the excess cellophane around the edge of the basket. If the arrangement is to be moved, tape the foam firmly in place.

2 To establish the overall shape of the arrangement, create a low dome of foliage with the tree ivy in proportion with the size and shape of the basket. Spread the tree ivy evenly throughout the plastic foam.

3 Wire the bunches of grapes by double-leg mounting on florist's wires. Position the bunches recessed in the foliage in a roughly diagonal line across the display. Handle the grapes delicately.

4 Push a wire through each fig from side to side, leaving projecting ends to bend downwards. Group the figs in pairs and push the wires into the plastic foam around the centre of the arrangement.

ABOVE: *Although there are many ingredients in this display, the spectacular final effect is well worth the extra attention.*

5 Emphasize the domed shape of the display with the antirrhinums, amaranthus and astilbe. Remove lower foliage and thorns from the roses, which are the focal flowers, and add them evenly through the display. To complete the arrangement, recess the hydrangea heads into the plastic foam, to give depth and texture. Water the foam daily to prolong the life of the display.

OLD-FASHIONED GARDEN ROSE POSY

*T*his tiny hand-tied posy of blown red and pale apricot roses and mint is designed to accompany a circlet headdress for a young bridesmaid. The velvet beauty of the contents gives it charm and impact.

MATERIALS
5 stems deep red and 5 stems pale
   apricot roses
scissors
20 stems mint
6 vine leaves
string
raffia

ABOVE: Finished with a natural raffia bow, the posy has a fresh, just-gathered look. Happily, it is very simple to make.

1 Remove all thorns and lower leaves from the rose stems. Starting with a rose in one hand, add alternately two stems of mint and one rose stem until all the materials are used. Keep turning the posy as you build, to form the stems into a spiral. Finally, add the vine leaves to form an edging to the arrangement and tie with string at the binding point (where the stems cross).

2 Trim the ends of the stems so that they are approximately one-third of the overall height of the posy. Tie raffia around the binding point.

TOPIARY ROSE TREE

This simple little double-headed tree makes a change from conventional arrangements. 'Yellow Dot' commercially grown spray roses open fully to a pretty rosette shape. The same design could be made up using dried rose-buds but you would need considerably more flowers and you would need to use plastic foam for dried flowers. Kept cool and frequently misted, this fresh rose tree should last for at least a week.

MATERIALS

2 spheres and 1 rectangular block
    plastic foam
knife
sturdy terracotta pot
3 bamboo canes
thick pliable string
secateurs
10 stems leucadendron
10 stems spray roses
sphagnum moss

1 *(Below left)* Soak the foam. Cut a piece of the rectangular block to fit in the pot. Insert the canes together and position the foam spheres on the canes. Bind the string around the canes.

2 *(Below right)* Cut off the leucadendron heads, leaving about 2 cm (¾ in) of stem, and insert into the foam spheres at regular intervals. Insert the roses in the same way. Cover the surface of the foam in the pot with sphagnum moss.

ABOVE: *For an effective rose tree select roses that open fully to provide a rosette shape. Remember to leave enough space around each rose for the bloom to open without being squashed.*

ROSE AND FRUIT BASKET

For a special dinner party or to decorate a side food table, this ornate moss-covered basket could contain either commercially grown or garden roses. Whichever roses you choose, it is important to select a sympathetically coloured fruit or berry to enhance the flowers. 'Prelude' is a commercially grown scented rose and its lilac tone is co-ordinated here with branches of small, immature purple plums and darker elderberry fronds. Crimson rose-hips and crab apples would look stunning with red, orange or yellow roses but for roses with a cream and white colouring, green fruits or vegetables, such as greengages and baby artichokes, would create a more effective result.

Dried poppy heads make a good contrast in shape to the roses.

MATERIALS
block plastic foam
knife
plastic bowl
string
sphagnum moss
wire basket
several small branches small plums and elderberry fruits
6 poppy seed-heads
8 stems roses
3 beeswax candles

WARNING: Never leave candles burning unattended.

BELOW: Rose-heads are less fragile and easier to manipulate when they are in bud, but allow enough room in the display for the blooms to open without disrupting the other elements.

1 Cut the foam to fit snugly in the bowl. Soak the foam in water until it is completely saturated. Wedge into the bowl and secure with string if the fit is not tight. Arrange the moss around the bowl to conceal it within the basket.

2 Make the initial shape of the arrangement using just the foliage and poppy heads.

3 Remove the lower foliage and thorns from the roses. Place the roses randomly, turning the basket to see the effect from all sides. Avoid putting the roses too close together. Then place the candles securely, making sure that no foliage or flowers will be near the flames.

ROSE AND HERB BASKET

Fresh flowers and herbs make a perfect partnership. The scent of the roses and herbs together is subtle but wonderful, especially if you hang the arrangement where you will brush lightly against it as you pass – but do not place it so that the roses are in danger of being crushed. If you do not have the herbs listed here, there are many alternatives, such as sage and rosemary and the leaves of any evergreen shrub.

MATERIALS
1 block plastic foam
small flower basket, with handle
plastic sheet
florist's adhesive tape
scissors
hellebore leaves
scented geranium leaves
12 small sprays golden oregano
12 stems cream roses

1 Soak the foam well. Line the basket with the plastic sheet, so that no water will seep through the basketwork. Put the foam block inside the liner and hold it in with tape. Cover the foam completely with a mixture of hellebore leaves and scented geranium leaves.

2 Add the sprays of golden oregano, placing them so that there will be room between them for the roses. Remove the lower foliage and any thorns from the roses. Place the roses evenly throughout the arrangement, putting six on each side of the handle so that the arrangement looks well balanced, but not too symmetrical. Top up the foam with water each day to prolong the life of the arrangement.

BELOW: A delightful country-style arrangement of roses and herbs brings the mingled scents of a summer garden into the house.

Apricot Roses and Pumpkins

The simple appeal of this design results from its use of just one type of flower and one type of foliage. The addition of tiny pumpkins gives body to the pretty combination of spray roses and flowering hypericum foliage. Note how the apricot colour is carried through flowers, pumpkins and container, complemented by the red buds and the yellow flowers of the hypericum.

MATERIALS
1 block plastic foam
knife
marble bird bath or similar container
florist's adhesive tape
scissors
10 stems hypericum
5 tiny pumpkins
florist's wires
10 stems apricot spray roses

1 Soak the block of plastic foam and cut it so that it can be wedged in place in the container. Secure the foam with florist's adhesive tape.

2 Create the outline of the display using the hypericum, and establish its overall height, width and length. The stems of commercially produced hypericum tend to be long and straight, with many offshoots of smaller stems. To create a more delicate foliage effect, and to get the most out of your material, use these smaller stems in the arrangement.

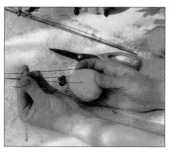

3 Wire each pumpkin by pushing one wire right through across the pumpkin base and out of the other side. Push another wire through to cross the first at right angles. Pull both wires down so that they project from the base. The pumpkins will be supported by pushing these wires into the plastic foam.

4 Position the pumpkins in the foliage, making sure that some are recessed more than others.

5 Remove any thorns and the lower foliage from the roses. Infill the arrangement with the spray roses. Like the hypericum, spray roses tend to have lots of small offshoots from the main stem and these should be used to get the most out of your materials. To augment the overall shape of the display, use buds on longer stems at the outside edges, with the most open blooms and heavily flowered stems in the centre.

OPPOSITE: *Substituting limes for the pumpkins will add a touch of vibrancy; for a more sophisticated look, use plums or black grapes.*

MINIATURE ROSES

A long-lasting gift for rose-lovers is *Rosa chinensis*, the pygmy or China rose. Modern miniature varieties of this species are available in flower all year round, and make a delightful alternative to cut flowers.

MATERIALS
wooden basket
plastic sheet
scissors
florist's adhesive tape
crocks
compost
3 miniature rose plants
sphagnum moss

1 Line the basket with a plastic sheet, securing it with florist's adhesive tape.

2 Arrange crocks over the base of the basket. Fill with compost.

3 Remove the rose plants from their pots and arrange them in the basket.

4 Pack moss into any spaces and cover the soil.

ABOVE: *Another idea is to make a fragrant* pot à fleurs, *using a basket that will hold a couple of miniature roses and a foliage plant.*

ABOVE: Other flowers and foliage that combine well with these tiny rose-heads need to be of a similar proportion, such as narcissi, lily of the valley, lavender, Nepeta mussinii, campanula or viola plants.

LEFT: Miniature roses planted in a long basket interspersed with herbs such as oregano, thyme or bush basil make an inside window-box for a kitchen or bathroom.

CELEBRATION TABLE DECORATION

A table for any celebratory lunch will not usually have much room to spare on it. In this instance there is no room for the wine cooler, and the answer is to incorporate this large, but necessary piece of catering equipment within the flower arrangement.

The floral decoration is a sumptuous, textural display of gold, yellow and white flowers with green and grey foliage. The spiky surfaces of the chestnuts add a wonderful variation in texture.

MATERIALS

40 cm (15 in) diameter plastic foam ring

scissors

25 stems Senecio laxifolius

15 stems elaeagnus

3 groups 2 chestnuts

florist's wires

thick gloves

18 stems yellow roses

10 stems cream-coloured Eustoma grandiflorum

10 stems solidago

10 stems flowering fennel

ABOVE: *The arrangement is based on a circular, plastic foam ring with the centre left open to accommodate the wine cooler. The splendid silver wine cooler is enhanced by the beauty of the flowers and, in turn, its highly polished surface reflects the flowers to increase their visual impact. This magnificent arrangement would make a stunning centrepiece for a wedding table.*

1 Soak the plastic foam ring in water. Cut the senecio to around 14 cm (5½ in) and distribute it evenly around the ring, leaving the centre clear.

4 Still wearing your gloves, arrange the groups of chestnuts at three equidistant points around the circumference of the plastic foam ring, and secure them by pushing the wires into the plastic foam.

5 Cut down the rose stems to approximately 14 cm (5½ in), remove lower foliage and any thorns and arrange in staggered groups of three roses at six points around the ring, equal distances apart, pushing the stems firmly into the plastic foam.

2 Cut the elaeagnus to a length of about 14 cm (5½ in) and distribute evenly throughout the senecio to reinforce the foliage outline, still leaving the centre of the plastic foam clear to accommodate the wine cooler.

3 Double-leg mount three groups of two chestnuts on wire and cut the wire legs to about 6 cm (2¼ in). Take care, as the chestnuts are very prickly and it is advisable to wear heavy-duty gardening gloves.

6 Cut stems of eustoma flower-heads 12 cm (4¾ in) long from the main stem. Arrange the stems evenly in the foam. Cut the stems of solidago to a length of about 14 cm (5½ in) and distribute throughout. Finally, cut the stems of fennel to about 12 cm (4¾ in) long and add evenly through the display, pushing the stems into the plastic foam.

VALENTINE'S HEART CIRCLET

ABOVE: *This takes a little more effort than ordering a bunch of flowers from your florist, but that effort will be seen as a measure of your devotion.*

*I*nstead of the traditional dozen red roses, why not give the love of your life a wall-hanging decoration for Valentine's Day?

Set your heart (in this case wooden) in a circlet of dried materials full of romantic associations – red roses to demonstrate your passion, honesty to affirm the truth of your feelings and lavender for the sweetness of your love.

MATERIALS
33 heads dried red roses
scissors
silver reel wire
florist's tape
55 stems dried lavender
10 stems dried honesty
florist's wires
1 small wooden heart, on a string

1 Cut the dried rose stems to approximately 2.5 cm (1 in) and individually double-leg mount on silver reel wires, then cover the stems with tape. Group three rose-heads together and double-leg mount on reel wire. Cover the stems with tape. Repeat the process for all the rose-heads, making in total eleven groups.

Group the dried lavender into bunches of five stems and double-leg mount on silver reel wire, then tape. Repeat the process for all the lavender, making eleven groups.

Cut pods from stems of dried honesty, group into threes and double-leg mount them on silver reel wires and tape. Make eleven groups.

Make a stay wire from florist's wires.

2 Lay a group of the honesty pods over one end of the stay wire and tape on securely. Then add, so that they just overlap, a group of lavender stems followed by a group of rose-heads, taping each group to the stay wire. Keep repeating this sequence, all the while bending the stay wire into a circle.

3 When the circle is complete, cut off any excess stay wire, leaving approximately 3 cm (1¼ in) to overlap. Then tape the two ends together through the dried flowers, to secure. Tie the string from the wooden heart on to the stay wire between the dried blooms, so that the heart hangs in the centre of the circlet.

HEART-SHAPED ROSE WREATH

This striking decoration uses a single type of rose in one colour.

MATERIALS
florist's wires
florist's tape
scissors
50 stems dried red roses
silver reel wire

1 Make a stay wire with florist's wires and tape. Form it into a heart shape about 22 cm (8¾ in) high, with the two ends of the wire meeting at its bottom point.

ABOVE: *This effective heart would make an unusual and long-lasting Valentine's Day gift.*

2 Cut the rose stems to about 2.5 cm (1 in). Double-leg mount them on silver reel wire and tape.

3 Starting at the top, tape the rose stems to the stay wire. Slightly overlap the roses to achieve a continuous line of heads, finishing at its bottom point. Starting back at the top, repeat the process around the other half of the heart. Tape the two ends of the wire together.

DOUBLE-HEART BASKET

This romantic flower basket, made from two interlocking hearts, is an intriguing present. The basic shape is moulded from fine wire mesh and covered in moss, to give it a fresh and natural appearance. One heart is packed with roses and the other piled high with strawberries for a summer-time treat – once the fruit has been eaten the basket could be filled with pot-pourri or small treasures.

MATERIALS
wire mesh
pliers
thick gloves
dried sphagnum moss
glue gun
1 block plastic foam for dried flowers
large bunch dried roses
scissors
fresh strawberries

2 Cover the hearts with handfuls of moss, using a glue gun to fix it in place. Press the moss right into the mesh, so that all of the wire is covered without losing the outline.

3 (Right) From the plastic foam, cut a heart shape to fit inside the left-hand heart and stick in place. Snip off the dried rose-heads and push a line of flowers into the edge of the foam.

4 Fill the centre space with more roses, placing them close together to form a padded cushion-like effect. Just before presentation, fill the second heart with strawberries.

1 Cut a 30 x 60 cm (12 x 24 in) piece of wire mesh. Halfway along, cut about 7.5 cm (3 in) into the wire at both top and bottom. Carefully mould the wire into two hearts, bending the mesh over to form a point at the bottom and two curves at the top. It is a good idea to wear gardening gloves while doing this.

ABOVE: *As an alternative to strawberries, you could fill the second basket with a selection of shells and berries.*

OPPOSITE: *Roses and hearts are natural partners for romantic gifts but in folk-art the heart is a symbol of friendship, making this a gift suitable for any occasion.*

SIMPLE POT OF ROSES

ABOVE: *A simple rose pot display can be made in single colours or, as here, with a combination. Make a matching pair to stand on a mantelpiece or shelf for a symmetrical, formal effect, or perhaps add a fabric bow for a softer, more romantic appearance.*

You do not need to wire the roses into bunches for this large pot. Instead, carefully place them in the foam one at a time, making sure that the rose-heads are well spaced, to create a good balance. You can add one or two other varieties of dried material to the display, if you like, but it will look most effective if the design is kept as simple as possible. When using roses alone in a large display, steam the heads open a little way before you start work. Bought flowers often look squashed and, as they are such an important part of this display, they should look their best. For a really stunning effect, use different combinations of size and colour, and try to retain as much of the green leaf as possible.

MATERIALS

terracotta pot
1 block plastic foam for dried
  flowers
knife
about 30 stems dried roses,
  in various colours
scissors
sphagnum moss
glue gun (optional)
florist's wires (optional)

1 Invert the pot and press to form an indentation on the foam block. Following the line the pot has made, cut off the excess foam with a sharp knife.

2 Trim the foam to fit the pot tightly and push in.

3 Press the foam firmly down into the pot; trim the top so that the foam and the top of the pot are level.

4 Trim each rose stem to the required length as you work. In the finished display, the roses should be at different levels so that the heads do not obscure or crowd each other.

6 Continue to press flowers into the pot; if you are using more than one colour, ensure that you have a good mix of hues over the display.

7 Finally, fix moss around the base of the roses with a glue gun, taking care not to burn yourself on the hot glue. Alternatively, bend short florist's wires over, to form U-shaped staples that can be pushed into the foam to trap the moss.

5 Start in the middle of the foam, pressing in the tallest rose. Then work outwards, continuing to add the stems one by one. Arrange the roses to any height, but make sure that they are a good balance for the size of the pot that you are using.

RIGHT: The colours of these peachy-pink and yellow roses are naturally offset by the subdued green moss and terracotta. Wherever possible, try to use antique terracotta pots, which have a pleasing texture and sympathetic look. If you can only obtain plastic pots, you can always conceal them in outer containers that reflect the colours of the display.

ROSE AND POTPOURRI GARLAND

This is a delicate and pretty garland, which uses a hop-vine ring as its base. These are fairly inexpensive and can be purchased ready-made from good florists. If you prefer, you could make your own, using vines or twigs cut when green so that they are pliable. Weave them together to form a ring and leave it to dry completely, when it will hold its shape.

MATERIALS
dried rose-heads
scissors
glue or glue gun
ready-made hop-vine or twig ring
sphagnum moss
potpourri
fir cones or woody material

ABOVE: *Although garlands are usually hung on a wall or door, they can be very effective as a table decoration, provided that they are not too large. Check that there are no pieces of wire sticking out from the back.*

1 Steam the heads of the roses to improve their appearance if necessary. Cut off the stems of the roses and glue the heads to the ring, some in pairs and others as single roses. Try to achieve a good balance. Next, glue hanks of moss to the ring in the gaps between the roses.

2 Now apply generous quantities of glue directly on to the ring and sprinkle on handfuls of potpourri, to cover the glue completely. Finally, add the fir cones or woody items, gluing them on to the ring singly or in pairs. Keep checking that all the material is well spaced. Work on the garland in sections and move the base ring around as you finish decorating each part.

RIGHT: *Try to keep the flowers and ingredients of this garland light and delicate. No decorative trimmings are really necessary but you could, perhaps, add a rustic trailing raffia bow.*

OLIVE OIL CAN ARRANGEMENT

2 Cut the dried roses so that they protrude about 10 cm (4 in) above the rim of the tin. Starting at the left-hand side of the tin, arrange a line of five tightly packed roses in the plastic foam from its front to its back. Continue arranging lines of five roses parallel to the first and closely packed across the width of the tin.

A n old olive oil can may not be the first thing to spring to mind when considering a container for your dried flower arrangement, but the bright reds, yellows and greens of this tin make it an attractive option.

Since this container is so striking, the arrangement is kept simple, using only one type of flower and one colour. This creates an effective contemporary display.

ABOVE: If you come across a nice container, however unlikely, remember it may be just right for a floral display. If you are using dried flowers it does not need to be watertight.

3 Continue adding lines of roses, until the roses are used up. Then take a small bundle of raffia about 3 cm (1¼ in) thick and twist it to make it compact. Loosely wrap the raffia around the stems of the roses just above the top of the tin and finish in a simple knot.

MATERIALS
1 block plastic foam for dried flowers
knife
small rectangular olive oil can
scissors
40 stems dried 'Jacaranda' roses
raffia

1 Cut the plastic foam to fit snugly in the olive oil can, filling it to 2 cm (¾ in) down from its rim.

SPRINGTIME CANDLE BOX

ABOVE: *Decorated candle boxes make ideal table centrepieces, which do not take up much room.*

This is a way of using gift boxes that are just too good to throw away. In this arrangement, an oval box is used. The candle shown is an option; a bigger box may need more than one candle to give the finished display a balanced look.

MATERIALS
glue gun
selection of leaves
box
scissors
1 block plastic foam for dried flowers
knife
candle
2 bunches miniature pink roses
florist's wires
sphagnum moss
raffia

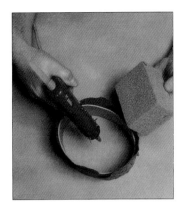

2 Using the knife, trim the foam block to the size of the box. Apply glue to the base of the foam block and push it firmly into the box. Try to create a good, tight fit; this will help to ensure that the box keeps its shape.

4 Trim the roses so that the finished length will allow around 3 cm (1¼ in) to be pushed into the foam, and around 5 cm (2 in) above the leaves. Insert the roses around the outside edge, spacing them to cover the whole surface. Leave space around the candle, so that there is no risk of the flowers burning. Cut short lengths of wire and bend them double into U-shaped pins, to attach the moss. Fill any space with moss. Trim the moss around the candle.

1 Spread a little glue on the back of each leaf and press each one of them firmly on to the side of the box. If the leaves are not large enough to cover the depth of the box, start the first row of leaves at the top and cover the bottom of the previous row with the next. Place the top row of leaves so that they extend well above the lip of the box. Carefully wipe away any excess glue.

3 When the glue has dried, push the candle firmly into the foam in the centre of the box to make a hole. Then remove the candle and put a small blob of glue in the hole. Put the candle back into the hole, making sure that it is straight. The glue will ensure that the candle is safe. The candle stub should come out easily if it is twisted gently; remember to glue the new candle in.

5 Tie raffia around the outside of the box.

WARNING: Never leave burning candles unattended.

ROSE AND STARFISH WREATH

ABOVE: *The construction of this wreath involves some wiring but is otherwise straightforward.*

The design of this visually simple wall decoration involves massing a single type of flower and framing them with a halo of geometric shapes, in this case, stars. The prettiness of its soft peach colours makes it suitable for a bedroom wall; if you are putting it in a bedroom, it is nice to sprinkle it with scented oil.

MATERIALS
10 small dried starfish
florist's wires
scissors
glue
13 cm (5 in) ring plastic foam for
    dried flowers
45 heads shell-pink dried roses
velvet ribbon

1 Double-leg mount the starfish as an extension of one of their arms, with a florist's wire. Cut the wire to about 2.5 cm (1 in) and apply glue to both the tip of the starfish arm and wire. Push the wired arm into the outside edge of the plastic foam ring. Position all the starfish around the ring. Leave a gap of about 3 cm (1¼ in) for attaching the ribbon.

2 Cut the stems of the rose-heads to about 2.5 cm (1 in) and put glue on their stems and bases. Push the glued stems into the plastic foam, to form a ring around its outside edge, on top of the starfish. Working towards the centre of the ring, continue forming circles of rose-heads until the ring is covered, apart from a gap for the ribbon.

3 Pass the ribbon through the centre of the ring and position it so that it sits in the gap between the roses and starfish, to cover the foam. This can be used to hang up the wreath or just tied in a bow for decoration.

$\mathscr{A}$ CROWN OF ROSES

There are many containers in the average household which, because of their colour, shape or material content, are suitable for a flower arrangement. This display was inspired entirely by the small crown-shaped, brass candleholder in which it is arranged.

An elevated position on, for example, a mantelpiece, would be perfect for such a small, neat display. Indeed, it could be used as a wedding-cake decoration.

MATERIALS
knife
1 block plastic foam for dried flowers
crown-shaped candleholder
scissors
15 stems poppy seed-heads
20 stems dried pink roses

ABOVE: *Making the display is straightforward and the method is applicable to any arrangement in a similarly small container.*

1 Cut a piece of plastic foam so that it can be wedged firmly into the candleholder, and sits about 2 cm (¾ in) below its top edge.

2 Cut the stems of the poppy seed-heads to 9 cm (3½ in) and push them into the foam, distributing them evenly to create a domed shape.

3 Cut the dried rose stems to 9 cm (3½ in) and push them into the foam between the poppy seed-heads, to reinforce the domed outline.

ROSE AND LAVENDER BASKET

This formal structure makes good use of three popular ingredients – roses, lavender and moss – and displays them to their best advantage in concentric rising patterns. Even stalks and waste leaves are used to dramatic effect. For this project, the basket was specially created from two rings fixed together with wire lengths – but a standard shallow round basket would work just as well.

MATERIALS

1 block plastic foam for dried flowers
knife
round basket
sphagnum moss
florist's wires
1 bunch dried lavender
scissors
about 25 stems dried red roses

1 Cut the foam to fit the basket and push in firmly. Make sure that the foam goes right to the edge and to the top of the basket.

2 Fix hanks of moss to the edge of the foam, so that it overlaps the top edge of the basket. Use florist's wires, bent double into U-shaped staples, to secure the moss in place.

3 Cut about 10–16 cm (4–6 in) off the bottoms of the lavender stalks. Wire them together at one end into even-size bunches, about 10 stalks per bunch. Press these in a circle into the foam, just inside the moss.

4 Wire up bunches of whole lavender in the same way, ensuring that they are of even height and that the flowers are level. Press carefully into the foam, to form an inner circle within the stalks, leaving a central circular space ready for the roses. Trim the roses and then wire into bunches of 2–3 flowers and insert into the centre.

RIGHT: *This staggered raised circle structure is well suited to a number of different ingredients – apricot roses and dried grasses, for instance, could be just as pleasing. When adding central roses, try to ensure that they are placed at an attractive angle, facing outwards, and that they retain as much of their foliage as possible. Ideally, when viewed from above, none of the foam should be visible through the flowers.*

Jam Jar Decorations

Containers decorated with plant materials can be very attractive. This type of external embellishment usually conceals a large part of the container, so do not waste money buying special pots and vases, just look around the house for something with an interesting shape that you can use.

Here, three different types and sizes of jam jars are decorated for use as night-light holders but they could be used to store pens or bric-à-brac or even in the bathroom for toothbrushes, although the damp will accelerate the deterioration of the materials.

Working on this scale does not use a great deal of material and is an opportunity to use leftover items or materials in some way unsuitable for flower-arranging. Use your imagination to vary the type of container and the flower decorations.

WARNING: Never leave candles burning unattended.

MATERIALS
floral adhesive
3 different-shaped jam jars
10 skeletonized leaves
scissors
18 heads dried yellow roses
3 night-lights
1 bunch dried lavender

ABOVE: *These decorations would make an unusual centrepiece for a dining table.*

1 Apply adhesive to the sides of the tallest jam jar (about 12 cm (4¾ in) high) and stick five upward-pointing leaves around the jar, flush with its base. Higher up the jam jar, glue on a second layer of leaves, slightly offset from the first layer.

2 Cut the stems off four dried yellow rose-heads and glue them to the jar at four equidistant points around the top of its outer surface. Place a night-light in the jar.

3 Cut the stems off 14 dried yellow rose-heads, apply floral adhesive to the base of each head and stick them around the neck of a more squat jar. Put a night-light in the jar.

4 Apply adhesive to the outside of the third jam jar. Separate the lavender into single stems and stick them vertically to the side of the jar, so that the flower spikes project about 1 cm (½ in) above its rim. The flower spikes should be tight to each other, to cover the sides of the jam jar. Apply a second layer of lavender spikes lower down. Trim the stems projecting below the jam jar flush with its base. Place a night-light in the jar, or use it as a small vase.

DRIED ROSE-HEAD CANDLE RING

*S*mall cane rings can be obtained from good florists but you could work with a length of hay rope instead, rather like a mini garland. Although any small-headed flower would be suitable for these decorations, dried roses are the perfect material. When the colours fade, spray on a frosting of gold or white paint to make Christmas candle rings. If you plan to use the decorations on tall candlesticks, make sure that you start the flowers well down the sides of the cane or hay ring, or the base and workings may be visible at eye-level to anyone nearby.

MATERIALS

glue gun
sphagnum moss
small cane ring or hay ring
scissors
8 heads dried roses
dried bupleurum
candle

1 Glue a light layer of moss to the cane or hay ring, making sure no glue is visible (it is white when set).

2 Cut all the roses from their stems, leaving as little stalk as possible, and begin to glue them into place. Position the roses carefully so that you maintain a symmetry in the design, unless that is you are deliberately aiming for a random, unstructured look. It is easiest to work on one side of the ring and then the other, to make sure the balance is right.

3 After you have added the roses, begin to fill in the spaces between them, using glue to fix the bupleurum in position. As you work make sure that the hole left in the middle will be large enough to take the candle. Fill any remaining gaps with more strands of moss. Finally, insert the candle in the ring.

ABOVE: *If you are using more than one shade or variety of rose on a candle ring, glue them in pairs of different colours and try to position the heads so that they are facing outwards.*

ABOVE: *This garland is made in the same way as the round candle ring, but you need a heart-shaped stay wire as your starting point.*

WARNING: Never leave candles burning unattended.

PARTY TABLE-EDGE SWAG

This is just about the simplest possible swag to make but, used as a table-edge decoration hanging in short loops, it gives an impressive finish to a festive table. Conifer boughs are inexpensive to buy and are freely available at any time of the year. You may have a suitable tree in your own garden, or be able to beg some from a friend.

This design is not long-lasting; the conifer will soon dry, become brittle and lose its vibrant green colour. If the swags need to be made a few days before the event, hang them in a cool, dry, dark place; this will ensure that the conifer stays looking good and this way there is plenty of time for other preparations. For a really fresh look, steam the roses gently to open them up.

MATERIALS
rope
fresh conifer
florist's reel wire
pale pink dried roses
scissors

1 Cut the rope to the required length and make a loop at each end. Trim the conifer to short lengths and remove any thorns and lower foliage from the roses. Bind the conifer to the rope, covering it all the way round, with reel wire.

2 Continue this process, adding the pink roses in twos and threes, with a handful of conifer stems at short intervals. Pack the conifer fairly tightly to produce a thick swag.

BELOW: Pale pink roses are used here for a summer party, but you could change the rose colour to give a different feel: red roses mixed with the conifer and used on a dark background would create a wintry look; for spring, pale yellow roses could be used.

DRIED ROSE TUSSIE MUSSIES

These tussie mussies are made of small spiralled bunches of lavender-scented dried flowers. Embellished with embroidered and velvet ribbon bows, they have a medieval look.

ABOVE: These tussie mussies are easy to make, although, to achieve a satisfactory result, they will use a lot of material in relation to their finished size.

2 Add, in turn, stems of *Nigella orientalis*, lavender and rose to the central stem. Continue this sequence, all the while turning the bunch in your hand to ensure that the stems form a spiral. Hold the growing bunch about two-thirds of the way down the stems (the binding point).

MATERIALS

Tussie Mussie A:
scissors
20 stems dried red roses
1 bunch dried Nigella orientalis
1 bunch dried lavender
string
ribbon

Tussie Mussie B:
scissors
20 stems dried pink roses
half-bunch nigella seed-heads
half-bunch dried lavender
half-bunch dried phalaris grass
string
ribbon

1 To make Tussie Mussie A, on the right of the main picture, cut all the materials to a stem length of approximately 18 cm (7 in). Set out all the materials in separate groups for easy access. Start by holding a single rose in your hand and add the other materials one by one.

3 When all the materials are in place, secure the bunch by tying string around the binding point of the stems. Trim the bottoms of the stems so they are even. Tie a ribbon around the binding point and finish in a neat bow. (Follow the same method for Tussie Mussie B.)

AUTUMNAL ROSE BUNDLE

This small display is one of the easiest to make, although it does have a fair number of steps. Dried roses, especially yellow or orange ones, will keep their colour for a very long time, so this makes an ideal design to fill a dark corner. Any combination of dried materials can be used. Raffia always gives a display a country feel; for a smarter location, the arrangement could be trimmed with a fabric bow.

BELOW: These flame-like roses make the arrangement suitable for autumn but you could vary the colours to suit any season or colour scheme.

MATERIALS

1 cylinder plastic foam for dried
flowers
brown paper
glue gun
knife
florist's wires
pliers
scissors
about 12 stems dried orange or
yellow roses
cobra or similar leaves
sphagnum moss (optional)
raffia

1 Place the foam cylinder in the centre of the brown paper and glue it in place. Cut from the edge of the foam to the outer edge of the paper, working all the way around at roughly 1 cm (½ in) intervals.

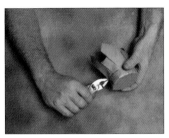

2 Fold the paper strips up. Wrap a florist's wire round the paper and the foam and twist the ends together.

3 Trim the paper in line with the top of the foam. Prepare and cut the rose stems, retaining as many leaves as possible. Starting in the centre, push them carefully one at a time into the foam.

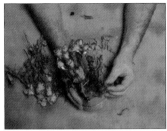

4 Continue the process until the whole of the foam has been covered with roses. If more leaves are required in the display, wire some bunches together and add them to the foam.

5 Fix three to four cobra leaves around the base with florist's wires bent into U-shaped staples.

6 Make sure all the pins are at the same height. Wrap a wire around the leaves at the same level as the pins and twist the ends together.

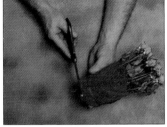

7 If the roses had a limited number of leaves, fill spaces around the stems with moss. Trim the leaves at the base of the display with scissors.

8 Tie raffia around the base, covering all the fixings, and finish with a bow or simple knot.

Dried rose tree

Without doubt, roses are among the most extravagant of flowers. In the same way that the powerful scent of an old garden rose can unexpectedly halt passers-by, so dried roses can be used in topiary designs to stunning effect.

MATERIALS

self-hardening clay

plant pot

straight twigs firmly tied together at the ends

plastic foam ball

10-12 bunches dried roses

scissors

florist's wires

small-headed filler flowers, such as achillea ('Lilac Beauty'), Achillea ptarmica ('The Pearl'), Alchemilla mollis, bupleurum, marjoram, oregano or solidago

sphagnum moss

1 Place the ball of clay in the pot and push the prepared twigs into the clay. Secure the plastic foam ball on top of the twigs. Trim the rose stems about 7.5–10 cm (3–4 in) from the base of the flower-head. This length will vary, depending on the size you want the finished tree to be.

2 Wire small bunches of 3–4 flowers together. You can also add the greenery at this stage, by trimming leaves from the waste stems and wiring this to the flowers. To create a perfect round, the flowers must align at the same level.

3 Push the wired bunches one at a time into the foam ball. Work in turn on one side and then another, building a basic shape all around the sphere. When you have added 10–12 bunches and you are satisfied with the shape, start to fill the spaces in between with your chosen filler flower. Always support the foam ball with a hand on the opposite side to where you are working.

4 When all the flowers are in place, there may still be gaps. Moss is excellent for filling any small spaces, as its rich dark green provides a perfect background for the flowers. Cut short lengths of wire and bend them into U-shaped pins, to fix the moss in place. To finish, cover the base of the trunk and the clay in the pot with generous handfuls of moss.

ABOVE: A tree of deep red and pale pink roses makes a stunning combination.

ABOVE: This rose tree has been sprayed with a fine coating of white paint to prolong its life.

DRIED ROSE WREATHS

These two wall-hanging decorations show how massed dried flowers in strong contrasting colours can create a striking contemporary display.

One display couples white roses with blue globe thistles, the second red roses with yellow roses; but alternative materials can be used, provided all the flower-heads used are about the same size. Consider green *Nigella orientalis* with white roses, bleached poppy seed-heads with bright yellow helichrysums or blue sea holly with orange carthamus.

MATERIALS

Red and Yellow Materials:
scissors
34 stems dried red roses
33 stems dried yellow roses
glue gun
10 cm (4 in) diameter plastic foam
   ring for dried flowers
ribbon

Blue and White Materials:
scissors
25 stems dried white roses
26 small heads echinops (blue globe
   thistle)
glue gun
10 cm (4 in) diameter plastic foam
ring for dried flowers
ribbon

RIGHT: *The wreaths are simple to make but will require a lot of material and a little patience to achieve the neat checkerboard patterns that characterize them.*

1 For the red and yellow wreath, cut the rose stems to about 2.5 cm (1 in). Around the outside edge of the plastic foam ring, form a circle of alternating yellow and red roses by gluing their stems and pushing them firmly into the foam. Leave a small gap in the rose circle for a ribbon. Inside the first circle, construct a second circle, offsetting the colours against the first ring.

2 Continue building circles of roses until the ring is covered. Pass the ribbon through the centre and around the gap on the plastic foam ring. Use the ribbon to hang the wreath or tie in a bow. Follow the same method for the second wreath.

DRIED FLOWER HAIR COMB

A decorated hair comb is a beautiful accessory for a special occasion and is particularly useful if the hair is worn up. This decoration in dried flowers is almost mono-chromatic, with creamy-white roses, silvery-grey eucalyptus, silvery-white honesty and soft green phalaris. Apricot-coloured dried starfish provide both colour and strong graphic shapes, which contrast with the softness of the flowers to create a stunning effect.

ABOVE: *Subtle colours and strong shapes make a lovely, unusual hair ornament for a party.*

MATERIALS
scissors
7 heads dried yellow roses
9 heads dried phalaris grass
fine-gauge florist's wires
3 small dried starfish
9 short stems eucalyptus
5 heads dried, bleached honesty
florist's tape
plastic hair comb

1 Cut the rose-heads and the phalaris to a stem length of 2 cm (¾ in), and double-leg mount them with florist's wire. Double-leg mount the small starfish with florist's wire. Cut two of the eucalyptus stems to a length of 6 cm (2¼ in) and the rest to about 4 cm (1½ in). Double-leg mount all the eucalyptus and individual heads of honesty with florist's wire. Cover the wired stems of all the materials with florist's tape. Create six units, two containing two roses, two with two phalaris and two with two eucalyptus stems, one at

6 cm (2¼ in) and one at 4 cm (1½ in), with the longer stem at the top of the unit.

2 Take two eucalyptus units and bind them together about 2 cm (¾ in) below the junction of the stems using florist's wire. At the binding point, bend each of the wired units away from each other, to form a straight line slightly longer than the length of the comb. Take all the units of rose and phalaris heads and bind them individually to the eucalyptus unit at the binding point. Bend each of them flat in the same way. Make all of these units slightly shorter than the eucalyptus.

ABOVE: *This special-occasion hair comb is quite intricate to construct but can be made in advance of the event, and the materials are available all year.*

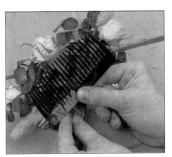

3 Place an individual rose-head at the centre of the bound units with the top about 5 cm (2 in) above the binding point. This will be the focal flower. Position the starfish and the honesty around this central rose-head and secure at the binding point with florist's wire. Wire in the individual heads of phalaris and short stems of eucalyptus.

4 Next, separate the wire stems below the binding point into two equal groups of wires, bend them apart and back on themselves, parallel to the main stems. Trim the wires at an angle to thin them out, before covering each group of wires with tape to create two wire prongs.

5 Lay these two wire prongs along the flat back of the comb and tape into position, by passing the tape between the teeth in the comb and around the wire prongs. Do this all the way along the length of the comb until the decoration is securely attached.

ROSE AND LAVENDER POSY

A bouquet always makes a welcome gift, but a bunch of carefully selected and beautifully arranged dried flowers will long outlast fresh blooms, to become an enduring reminder of a happy occasion. The "language of flowers" interprets the meaning of lavender as "devoted attention" and the pink rose as a symbol of affection, so this posy should really only be made for a very special friend.

MATERIALS
florist's wires
12 large artificial or glycerined leaves
florist's tape
1 bunch dried lavender
1 bunch dried rose-buds
paper ribbon

ABOVE: *The soft colours of lavender and dried roses make this a striking arrangement.*

1 Fold a florist's wire one-third of the way along its length, to form a 15 cm (6 in) stalk. Attach a leaf to the top by its stalk and tape in place, wrapping the tape down to the end of the wire. Repeat to prepare 12 leaves.

2 Divide the lavender into several small bunches. Hold them together loosely, setting the bunches at an angle to each other to give a good shape. This will form the basic structure of the posy.

3 Taking a single rose-bud at a time, push the stems into the lavender, spacing them out evenly.

4 If desired, bind the posy with florist's wire at the binding point (where the stems cross) so it will keep its shape while you work. Then edge the posy with the wire-mounted leaves. Bind in place again.

5 Unravel the paper ribbon and use to bind all the stalks together tightly, covering the wire and the stalks completely. Finish off by tying the ends of the ribbon into a bow.

OPPOSITE: *Lavender and roses are a popular combination with flower arrangers.*

COUNTRY ROSE POT

This simple pot of rural roses has a pleasing dishevelled appearance, emphasized by the layer of hay attached to the outside of the terracotta pot. It is trimmed with a large loose raffia bow and would look wonderful on a traditional dresser or kitchen cabinet.

MATERIALS
knife
1 block plastic foam for dried flowers
terracotta pot
florist's reel wire
glue or glue gun (optional)
hay
scissors

1 bunch dried red roses
1 bunch dried poppy seed-heads
raffia

BELOW: *To ensure that the roses retain their colour, keep the display out of direct sunlight. If the flowers or poppy heads become a little dusty, brush them clean with a dry paintbrush.*

1 Cut the foam block with a knife to fit the pot and press firmly in. Tightly wrap reel wire 2–3 times around the pot near the top. If you have a glue gun, you could glue the wire to anchor it firmly to the pot.

2 Lay the pot on its side and wire on the hay in generous amounts. Do not worry if the hay is uneven, it will be trimmed later. As you add the hay, trap it tightly under the wire, or take the wire completely around the pot each time you add a new bundle.

3 When the pot is covered, tie the wire tightly. If you wish to be certain that the hay will not come off, glue around the pot over the wire and into the hay. Now trim the hay to expose the base of the pot. Pull off any loose strands. Do not trim the top but remove any straggly pieces. You should aim to get the hay looking fairly tidy, but do not spend too long fussing over it. The whole design will be transformed once you have started to add the flowers.

ABOVE: *This variation of the Country Rose Pot shows how easy it is to achieve a different feel by changing the colour of the roses. Here country-style ingredients create a pretty, casual display. You could also replace the raffia bow with a fabric or paper one, for a more sophisticated look.*

4 Separate the roses and poppies and wire them in groups of 3–4 into small bunches, although you might find it easier to work with individual, single stems. The heads need to show above the top of the hay collar, so remember to leave enough length on the stems to push into the foam. Fill the centre of the pot with the roses and poppy heads, making sure that you have a good balance of colour and form. Finally, tie a raffia bow around the pot to cover the wire that is fixing the hay. Try to make the loops of the bow well rounded and generous in size. Trim any unwanted raffia from the ends as necessary.

TRADITIONAL TIERED BASKET

This regimented formal design can be very effective and is one of the easiest for beginners to perfect. So long as you make sure that each layer of materials is the correct height, you should make a dramatic display, the loose and flowing ingredients combining well within the confines of a disciplined structure.

MATERIALS
knife
1 block plastic foam for dried flowers
rectangular basket
dried flowers and foliage such as
*   wheat, lavender, roses*
scissors or cutters
sphagnum moss
florist's wires

2 Lavender (wired into small bunches of 5–6 stems) is pushed into the foam directly in front of the wheat. Arrange the stems so that the lavender flowers come to just below the heads of wheat. Make sure the flowers are all facing the same way, to achieve symmetry.

3 Add the roses next, positioning them individually in front of the row of lavender. Try to keep as much foliage as space will allow, but be prepared to cut away a fair amount from each stem. Place the roses at slightly varying heights, so that each flower head is visible.

1 Cut the foam block to fill the basket and press firmly in. Start in the centre of the foam with the tallest ingredient (wheat in this case), wired into bunches of 8–10 stems. Pack the stems closely together, to achieve a good density. Check that the height balances visually with the size of the basket.

4 Complete the display by covering the foam at the base with generous handfuls of moss. Fix this in place with short lengths of florist's wires bent into U-shapes. Remember that fresh moss shrinks a little when it dries, so allow it to overhang the sides of the basket at this stage.

ABOVE: *This simple, structured display is most effective when created as a flat-backed piece, which can be placed against a wall or perhaps used to fill a fireplace during the summer months. It is also particularly well suited for window sills – the wheat will shield the flowers in front from strong sunlight so they will last for longer before their colours fade.*

Dried Rose Baby Gift

What could be nicer for new parents than to receive a floral symbol of good luck on the birth of their baby? The whites and pale green of this dried-flower horseshoe make it a perfect, delicately coloured decoration for the nursery.

MATERIALS
14 heads dried white roses
42 heads dried bleached honesty
60 heads dried phalaris grass
scissors
silver reel wire
florist's tape
florist's wires
ribbon

2 Make a stay wire approximately 30 cm (12 in) long from florist's wire and florist's tape.

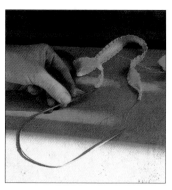

4 Form the stay wire into a horseshoe shape. Tape one wired end of the ribbon to one end of the stay wire. Tape one of the bows over the junction of the ribbon and stay wire, making sure it is securely in place.

1 Cut the rose stems, honesty stems and phalaris grass to approximately 2.5 cm (1 in) long. Double-leg mount the roses individually on silver reel wire, then tape. Double-leg mount the phalaris heads in groups of five, and the honesty in clusters of three, on silver reel wire. Tape each group.

3 Form three small bows about 4 cm (1½ in) wide from the ribbon and bind them at their centres with silver reel wire. Cut a 30 cm (12 in) length of ribbon and double-leg mount both ends separately with silver reel wire. This will form the handle for the horseshoe.

5 Tape the flowers and foliage to the stay wire, to its mid-point, in the following repeating sequence: phalaris, rose, honesty. Tape a bow at the centre. Tape the last bow and the remaining ribbon end to the other end of the stay wire. Work the flowers in the same sequence to the centre point.

OPPOSITE: *While making the horseshoe is relatively time consuming, the effort will no doubt have created something of such sentimental value that it will be kept forever. An occasional dusting with a fine paintbrush will help to keep it looking good.*

Old-Fashioned Garden Rose Corsage

This delicate rose corsage would provide the perfect finishing touch for that special wedding or summer ball outfit. However, it has to be remembered that old-fashioned garden roses are really only available in the summer months.

MATERIALS

8 stems rose leaves

scissors

3 heads roses, graded thus: in bud, just open, fully open

3 small vine leaves

florist's silver wires

florist's tape

ABOVE: *Using just one type of flower, with its own foliage, and three individual leaves ensures the result is simple yet elegant.*

1 Cut the stems of the rose leaves to the following lengths: two at 6 cm (2¼ in), two at 4 cm (1½ in), four at 3 cm (1¼ in). Cut the rose-head stems to 4 cm (1½ in). Remove lower foliage and any thorns. Cut the vine leaf stems to 2.5 cm (1 in) and stitch-wire with florist's silver wire.

Make two "units" of rose leaves, each with one 6 cm (2¼ in) stem and one 4 cm (1½ in) stem. Make another unit using the two smaller rose-heads.

2 Hold one unit of rose leaves in your hand and place the unit of rose- heads on top, so that the leaves project slightly above the upper rose-head. Bind the units together with silver wire, 6 cm (2¼ in) below the lower rose-head.

Add the second unit of rose leaves lower and to the left of the first. Add the fully opened rose (the focal flower) with the top of its head level with the bottom of the rose above. Bind to the corsage.

Position the vine leaves around the focal flower and bind in place. Position the remaining individual rose leaves, slightly recessed, around the focal flower and bind in place.

3 Trim off the ends of the wires approximately 5 cm (2 in) below the focal flower and cover with tape. Adjust as desired.

ABOVE: *Commercially grown roses make an equally elegant corsage when garden roses are not available. Pick the colours carefully to complement the outfit.*

DRIED ROSE AND APPLE BUTTONHOLE

Dried flowers can also come into their own at weddings, though fresh ones are more usual. The advantages are that the bride can keep her flowers after the event and it may be a practical measure for a winter wedding, where fresh flowers are unavailable or expensive. This buttonhole is designed to be worn by a groom or best man and, unusually, incorporates fruit with the flowers and foliage.

MATERIALS

3 slices preserved apples
florist's wires
scissors
6 stems dried roses
6 short stems glycerined eucalyptus
1 small head dried hydrangea
florist's tape
silver reel wire

ABOVE: *Apple slices give texture and a light touch to the decoration. Add a few drops of rose oil to give scent if you wish.*

1 Double-leg mount the apple slices together on florist's wire. Trim each rose stem to 2.5 cm (1 in) and wire. Double-leg mount the roses in two groups of three. Leave a 5 cm (2 in) stem on the eucalyptus and hydrangea and double-leg mount on florist's wires. Tape all the elements.

2 Hold the rose-heads in your hand and place the apple slices behind. Then position the hydrangea to the left and bind together all the stems using silver reel wire. Position the eucalyptus stems to frame the edge of the buttonhole and bind with silver reel wire.

3 When all the elements are bound securely in place, cut the wired stems to a length of approximately 5 cm (2 in) and bind them with florist's tape. Adjust the wired components until you achieve the desired shape, not forgetting the profile.

YELLOW ROSE BUTTONHOLE

The bold choice of vibrant colours characterizes this stunning buttonhole. The yellow roses and elaeagnus, the orange-red rose-hips and lime green fennel combine to produce a simple, visually strong decoration suitable for either a man or a woman.

MATERIALS
scissors
1 stem yellow rose
florist's wires
5 elaeagnus leaves, graded in size
florist's silver wires
15 rose-hips and leaves
1 head fennel
florist's tape
silver reel wire
pin

ABOVE: *As with all buttonholes, the construction involves wiring which is, of course, time-consuming. Make sure you leave plenty of time to create buttonholes on the day they are needed.*

1 Cut the rose stem to 4 cm (1½ in), remove any thorns and wire. Stitch-wire all the elaeagnus leaves with silver wires. Group the rose-hips, on stems of 4 cm (1½ in), in bunches of five and wire with silver wires. Divide the head of fennel into its component stems and wire in small groups with silver wires. Tape all the wired elements.

2 Keeping the rose-head central to the display, bind the bunches of fennel and rose-hips around it, with silver reel wire. Bind the elaeagnus leaves to the arrangement with silver reel wire, placing the largest leaf at the back of the rose, the two smallest at the front, and two medium-sized leaves at the side.

3 Trim the wires to approximately 7 cm (2¾ in) and tape the wires with florist's tape. Look closely at the completed buttonhole, and, if necessary, bend the leaves down to form a framework for the rose and adjust the overall shape so that the back of the decoration is flat for pinning to the lapel.

CIRCLET HEADDRESS
FOR A YOUNG BRIDESMAID

Although classic in its design, this bridesmaid's circlet head-dress is given a contemporary feel by the use of a rich colour combination not usually associated with traditional wedding flowers.

MATERIALS
9 heads deep red roses
9 small clusters apricot spray roses
8 small bunches rose-hips
scissors
florist's wires
9 small individual vine leaves
florist's silver wires
florist's tape
9 small bunches mint

ABOVE: The small bunches of orange-red rose-hips give a substance to the fabric-like texture of the red and apricot coloured roses.

1 Cut all the flowers to a stem length of approximately 2.5 cm (1 in) and remove any rose thorns. Wire the individual rose-heads with florist's wires. Stitch-wire the vine leaves with silver wire. Tape all the wired items.

2 Make a stay wire with florist's wires about 4 cm (1½ in) longer than the circumference of the head. Tape the wired flowers and foliage to the stay wire in the following repeating sequence: individual rose, mint, spray rose, vine leaf, rose-hips.

3 As you tape materials to the stay wire, form it into a circle. Leave 4 cm (1½ in) of the stay wire undecorated, overlap it behind the beginning of the circlet and tape securely together through the flowers.

DRIED FLOWER GARLAND HEADDRESS

This wedding headdress is made from dried materials in beautiful soft pale pinks, greens and lilacs with the interesting addition of apple slices. Apart from being very pretty, it will not wilt during the wedding.

MATERIALS
scissors
9 heads dried peonies with leaves
27 heads dried red roses
florist's wires
silver wires
silver reel wire
27 slices preserved apple
18 short sprigs ti tree
9 small clusters dried hydrangea
9 stems eucalyptus
florist's tape

1 Cut the peonies and the roses to a stem length of 2.5 cm (1 in). Double-leg mount the peonies with florist's wires and the roses with silver wires. Group the roses into threes and bind together using the silver reel wire. Group the apple slices into threes and double-leg mount them together with wire. Cut the sprigs of ti tree, hydrangea clusters and eucalyptus to lengths of 5 cm (2 in) and double-leg mount with silver wires, grouping the ti tree and eucalyptus in twos. Cover all the wired stems with tape.

2 Have to hand the bride's head measurements. Make the stay wire on which the headdress will be built using florist's wires, ensuring its final length is approximately 4 cm (1½ in) longer than the circumference of the wearer's head.

3 Position a piece of wired eucalyptus on one end of the stay wire and wrap florist's tape over its stem and the stay wire, to secure them together. Then, in the same way, add in turn a hydrangea cluster, a group of roses, a peony and a group of ti tree, repeating the sequence until the stay wire is covered. Remember to leave the last 4 cm (1½ in) of the stay wire uncovered.

4 To complete the headdress, overlap the uncovered end of the stay wire with the decorated end and tape together with florist's tape, ensuring the tape goes under the flowers so that it is not visible.

OPPOSITE: *The bold nature of this headdress makes it particularly suitable for a bride.*

SIMPLE WEDDING BOUQUET

ABOVE: *The bouquet needs to stand in water for as long as possible before the big event, but dry the stems carefully before it is carried by the bride!*

A simple bunch of freshly picked flowers is the most traditional form of flower arrangement and its natural beauty is the fashion for most modern brides. Rather than the tortured wiring of every stem, the flowers are arranged in the hand, creating a spiral effect by placing the stalks in one direction. This style of arrangement, known as the hand-tied or continental bouquet, is very popular in Europe, particularly in the Netherlands where it was first developed. Unlike the old-fashioned flat or sheaf bouquets, in which all the stems are of differing lengths, the hand-tied bouquet is ready to go straight into a vase without any further arranging. The linear hand-tied bouquet is a very romantic arrangement, perfect for brides with long flowing dresses. It may be held either pointing downwards or in the curve of an elbow. Yellow and white flowers are synonymous with spring and several branches of mimosa add a sharp, sweet fragrance to the bouquet.

MATERIALS

5 stems commercially grown spray roses 'Yellow Dot'
5 stems commercially grown spray roses 'Tina'
5 stems mimosa
5 stems variegated pittosporum
5 stems pale yellow tulips 'Montreux'
5 stems white tulips 'Casablanca'
5 stems white anemone
5 stems trailing variegated ivy
string or raffia
scissors
white or pale yellow ribbon

1 Strip all the flowers and foliage leaves and thorns which would be below the binding point, about a third of the way up each stem. Thorns should be neatly cut off so as not to damage the rose stems. Place a rose, a stem of mimosa and one of pittosporum in one hand to form the centre of the bouquet.

2 With the other hand lay each subsequent stem at a 45° angle, always in the same direction. Turn the bouquet in the hand so that a spiral gradually develops. Hold the stems firmly at the binding point while adding new flowers.

3 Twist the string or raffia just above the hand and then take it up and around the stems and tie. With sharp scissors, trim all the stems to size, leaving a long slant at the end. Tie with ribbon.

HAND-TIED BOUQUET

ABOVE: *Brightly coloured ribbon that matches the flowers or the dress covers the raffia or string. This posy is easily kept in water before it is carried and may be made the day before the wedding, to allow some of the flowers to start to open.*

This jewel-coloured hand-tied bouquet is perfect for the less conventional bride or for those being married in winter who prefer bright tones. Make smaller versions for the bridesmaids. Flowers have traditionally been used to symbolize emotions and the use of the floral language was very popular in Victorian times when specific flowers were worn as a discreet form of communication between the sexes. The language of flowers is still observed by some brides when they choose their bouquet and, since the rose is associated with love, it is by far the most popular.

MATERIALS

7 stems commercially grown rose 'First Red'
5 stems commercially grown rose 'Ecstasy'
5 stems commercially grown rose 'Leonardis'
5 stems commercially grown rose 'Konfetti'
7 stems orange ranunculus (turban buttercup)
5 stems viburnum
5 stems liquidambar (sweet gum)
5 stems cotinus (smoke bush)
scissors
string or raffia
ribbon

1 Prepare the ingredients by stripping off most of the rose leaves and all of those on the ranunculus and viburnum. Snip off all the rose thorns. Begin with a rose stem and lay a ranunculus stem over it.

2 Holding the stems upright, gradually add more stems to the bouquet at a 45° angle, turning the bouquet around in your hand as you work, to create the spiralling effect.

3 Once you are satisfied with the overall size and shape of the bouquet tie the stems together with string or raffia. Trim the stems and finish off with a coloured ribbon.

THE LANGUAGE OF ROSES

Deep red rose   *Simplicity and beauty*
Red rose   *Eternal love*
Red rose-buds   *Pure and lovely*

White rose   *Truth*
Single rose   *Simplicity*
White and red roses   *Unity*

BRIDE'S VICTORIAN POSY WITH DRIED FLOWERS

Traditionally, the Victorian posy took the form of a series of concentric circles of flowers. Each circle contained just one type of flower, with variations only from one circle to the next. Such strict geometry gives formal-looking arrangements particularly suitable for weddings.

MATERIALS

scissors
11 heads white roses
18 heads pink roses
3 heads dried pink peonies
florist's wires
12 stems glycerined eucalyptus,
  approximately 10 cm (4 in) long
63 heads dried phalaris grass
12 clusters dried honesty, with 5
  heads in each cluster
florist's silver wires
12 small bunches dried linseed
10 small clusters dried hydrangea
florist's tape
silver reel wire
ribbon

1 Cut the roses and peonies to a stem length of 3 cm (1¼ in) and single-leg mount them on florist's wires. Cut the eucalyptus stems to 10 cm (4 in). Remove the bottom leaves, then wire as for roses and peonies.

Double-leg mount the phalaris grass and honesty heads on silver wire in groups of five. Single-leg mount these groups on wires to extend their stem lengths to 25 cm (10 in). Repeat the process with groups of linseed and hydrangea. Tape all wired elements with florist's tape.

2 Arrange the three peony heads around a white rose head. Bind together with silver reel wire, starting 10 cm (4 in) down the stems.

3 Rotating the growing posy in your hand, form a circle of pink rose-heads around the peonies and bind to the main stem. Around this, form another circle, this time alternating white rose-heads and clusters of hydrangea, and bind. Each additional circle of flower-heads will be at an increasing angle to the central flower, to create a dome shape.

4 Next add a circle of phalaris grass to the posy, followed by a circle of alternating honesty heads and linseed. Bind each circle with silver reel wire at the binding point as it is completed.

5 Finally, add a circle of eucalyptus stems and bind with tape. The eucalyptus leaves will form a border to the posy and cover any exposed wires underneath.

6 To form a handle, place the bundle of bound wires diagonally across your hand and trim off any excess wires. Tape with florist's tape and cover the handle with ribbon.

YELLOW ROSE BRIDESMAID'S BASKETS

ABOVE: *The flowers are secured in plastic foam and will remain lovely and fresh, for the bridesmaid to take away and keep after the wedding.*

These arrangements will keep young bridesmaids happy on two counts: first, they are easier to carry than posies and, second the simple bright colours are such fun – sunshine yellow roses and lime green fennel in a basket stained orange-red.

MATERIALS
For each basket you will need:
half-block plastic foam
knife
1 small basket, plastic-lined
florist's adhesive tape, if necessary
scissors
30 stems birch, approximately 10 cm
(4 in) long
10 stems yellow roses
5 stems fennel
raffia

1 Soak the plastic foam in water and cut it with a knife to wedge firmly in the basket. (If you are using a shallow basket, you may need to secure the foam in place with florist's adhesive tape.)

2 Clean the leaves from the bottom 3 cm (1¼ in) of the birch stems. Arrange them in the plastic foam, creating an even, domed outline.

3 Cut the roses and fennel to a stem length of 8 cm (3¼ in) and remove any thorns. Distribute evenly throughout the birch stems.

4 Tie a raffia bow at the base of the handle on both sides and trim to complete the display.

$\mathcal{Y}$ELLOW ROSE BRIDESMAID'S POSY

$\mathcal{A}$ posy made from slim-stemmed materials has a narrow binding point which makes it easier to carry. This posy uses such materials in a simple but striking combination of yellow roses, lime green fennel and delicate green birch leaves.

MATERIALS
20 stems yellow roses
scissors
5 stems fennel
15 stems birch leaves
twine
raffia

ABOVE: Easy to make as a hand-held, spiralled bunch and finished with a natural raffia bow, this posy would be a delight for any bridesmaid to carry and enjoy.

1 Strip all but the top 15 cm (6 in) of the rose stems clean of leaves and thorns. Split the multi-headed stems of fennel until each stem has one head only. This makes them easier to handle and visually more effective in the posy. Strip all but the top 15 cm (6 in) of the birch stems clean of leaves.

2 Holding one rose in the hand, add individual stems of fennel, birch and rose in a continuing sequence, all the while turning the bunch to spiral the stems. Continue until all the materials are used.

3 Tie the posy with twine at the binding point – the point where the stems cross. Trim the bottom of the stems to leave a stem length of approximately one-third of the overall height of the finished display. Complete the posy by tying raffia around the binding point and finishing with a bow. Finally, trim the ends of the raffia.

ROSE CRAFTS

Roses offer an abundance of materials
and ideas for creating both lovely and
useful things for gifts or display. The following
pages show inspirational ideas to suit crafts-
people and cooks of all abilities.

ROSE CANDLES

ABOVE: *Church candles are best for decorating as they have a high proportion of beeswax and therefore burn for longer. They also soften and then harden more quickly than cheap paraffin wax.*

Candlelight is still the most romantic and flattering artificial light you can create. It enhances food, cunningly hides any dust or flaws in the room and makes faces look warm and glowing. Scented candles imbue a gentle fragrance as they burn but you should buy the better-quality examples, as cheaper versions use synthetic and often overpowering scents. A few drops of essential oil can be added to the melted pool of wax as the candle is burning for the same effect.

Aromatic burners give you the option of mixing different oils together or varying the oil if you so desire. A purpose-made dish is gently warmed by a night-light placed underneath and, as the oil evaporates, it releases its fragrance into the surrounding atmosphere. A home-made version can be improvized by placing drops of essential oil in a saucer and leaving it on top of a warm radiator.

Decorating candles is easy and the effect can be stunning. Rose-heads and leaves can be applied as decoration and each time the candle is dipped the flower or leaf is sealed more deeply into the candle. Heavier decorations take more practice: speed is crucial if it is to stick before the wax hardens.

WARNING: Never leave burning candles unattended.

MATERIALS
deep, narrow saucepan
church candle, preferably one of the shorter and fatter shapes
pressed rose-heads
selection of small silver metal shapes, such as stars
flat beads or buttons
tweezers

1 Fill the saucepan with boiling water. Dip one end of the candle into the water for 4–5 seconds. Remove from the water quickly and stick on as many of the pressed rose-heads and other decorations as you can before the wax hardens.

2 Repeat the process, turning the candle each time and not leaving it in the water for too long. A pair of tweezers may help to push the heavier items into the wax.

ROSE AND PRESSED-FLOWER GIFT WRAP

Specially made wrapping and decoration can make any present more enticing. This novel wrapping conceals an exciting surprise – pressed flowers between the wrapping paper and the box.

MATERIALS
cardboard box
tissue paper
pressed flowers
handmade paper with petals
string
sealing wax
dried roses
gift tag

RIGHT: This idea can be adapted to suit any occasion, by varying colours and materials.

1 Cover the box with several layers of tissue paper. Scatter pressed flowers on the top, before wrapping around the handmade paper.

2 Tie a double length of string around the parcel, finishing off with a bow. Drip sealing wax on to the string, to hold it in place.

3 Tuck three dried roses under the string and tie a gift tag on to the bow to complete the parcel.

ROSE GIFT TAGS AND BOXES

The presentation of a gift adds the finishing touch which can transform a very simple and modest item into something exciting. Careful selection of paper and trimmings show just how much thought and time has been taken for the recipient and these sentiments are always thoroughly appreciated. Even brown paper can be sprayed with an alcohol-based perfume and tied with raffia made into an exuberant bow securing a small bunch of rosebuds.

Some gifts are difficult to wrap: they are unruly shapes or so obvious in shape a degree of disguise is needed to keep the recipient guessing. Collect boxes for this purpose, such as shoe boxes. These can be covered with gift wrap and padded with layers of tissue.

Decorative rubber stamps dipped in colourful inks change plain papers into decorated wrapping. The soft ribbons found on haberdashery counters are much more luxurious than those sold in stationery shops. Gold and silver metallic stars can be stuck to plain papers for a glittery effect and also sprinkled inside the wrapping, to create an unexpected shower as the present is opened.

GIFT TAGS

MATERIALS
rose-heads or petals
rose leaves
blotting paper
flower press or heavy books
paper glue
coloured card or blank gift tag
inset paper (optional), such as
*   handmade or textured*
hole punch
raffia or fine string

2 After several weeks, the flowers and leaves should be completely dry, wafer-thin and very fragile. Do not be surprised if some of the original colours have either darkened or faded while drying.

1 To press rose-heads and petals, carefully place them face down on blotting paper. Cover any spaces with leaves of a similar thickness, taking care not to squash the flowers or overlap them. Cover with a layer of blotting paper and press for several weeks. If you do not have a flower press, several heavy books will work just as well.

3 Using paper glue, stick the leaves and flowers in a design on coloured card or gift tag, or for a layered effect, use a paler or white inset paper. For a rough "torn" edge, moisten the paper and gently tear the shape you want.

4 *(Left)* Punch a hole in the card or gift tag and thread through a long, thin piece of raffia or fine string. Use this to tie to the packet.

ABOVE: Use dried roses to decorate wrapped presents, and pressed rose petals on your gift tags; rose motifs are also delightfully decorative.

*G*IFT BOX

A decorated gift box enhances the pleasure of a gift and also makes it intriguingly difficult to guess what is inside. Roses are a marvellous decorative motif and are particularly delightful for decorating a romantic present, especially one for Valentine's Day. The glittering stars and crescents on this gift box also make it suitable for wrapping a Christmas present.

MATERIALS
cardboard box
plain white paper
all-purpose glue
metallic stars and crescents
ribbon
dried rose-buds

1 Cover a box with plain white paper. Using all-purpose glue, squeeze dots over the top and sides and scatter metallic stars and crescents. Shake off the loose shapes.

3 (Right) Attach a tiny posy of roses to the knot with more of the same ribbon. Finish off by tying the remainder of the ribbon in a bow.

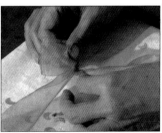

2 Cut a piece of contrasting ribbon to length and tie around the box, knotting it in the centre of the lid.

MASSED ROSE STAR DECORATION

This display has a huge visual impact of massed colour and bold shapes with the added bonus of the delicious scent of lavender.

Built within a star-shaped baking tin and using yellow and lavender colours, the display has a very contemporary appearance. It would suit a modern interior.

MATERIALS
2 blocks plastic foam for dried flowers
knife
star-shaped baking tin
scissors
500 stems dried lavender
100 stems dried yellow roses

RIGHT: This decoration is simple to make, although it does call for a substantial amount of roses.

1 Cut the plastic foam so that it fits neatly into the baking tin and is recessed about 2.5 cm (1 in) down from its top. Use the tin as a template for accuracy when cutting the foam blocks.

2 Cut the lavender stems to 5 cm (2 in) and group them into fives. Push the groups into the plastic foam all around the outside edge of the star shape, to create a border of approximately 1 cm (½ in).

3 Cut the dried roses to 5 cm (2 in). Starting at the points of the star and working towards its centre, push the rose stems into the foam. All the heads should be level with the lavender flowers.

ROSE NAPKIN RINGS

Almost any type of large, preserved leaf can be used alongside roses to make these napkin rings. Preserved leaves often have dye added to the preserving liquid, which can sometimes rub off the leaf, leaving a stain. Before working with the material, give it a gentle rub with a light-coloured cloth to see if this happens (darker coloured leaves cause the most problems). Red roses are used here, but you can vary the colour to match your table setting.

MATERIALS
cobra leaves
glue gun
red roses
green moss

RIGHT: Home-made napkin rings add a special charm to a table setting and, of course, can be made to co-ordinate with any other floral table and room decorations.

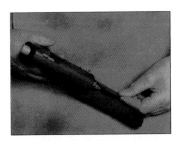

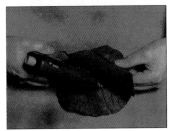

1 *(Above left)* Roll a leaf to form a tube, glue the edge down and hold it until it sets.

2 *(Below left)* Glue the tube-shaped leaf to a flat leaf along its centre spine. Choose a leaf that is about the same length as the rolled leaf.

3 *(Above right)* Either side of the rolled leaf, glue two red roses. If they are rather small, glue more than two or steam them to make them look larger.

4 *(Below right)* Trim with a little green moss, glued in place.

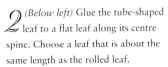

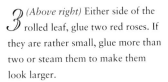

ROSE BUTTONHOLES AND CORSAGES

It used to be the fashion for gentlemen to present their ladies with an elaborate corsage of scented flowers to wear on a special occasion such as a grand ball. This custom is now mainly restricted to wedding guests wearing boring carnations with a sprig of asparagus fern as buttonholes. With imagination and a little skill and expenditure, though, it is quite possible to create some really attractive arrangements to wear for formal occasions, such as weddings or other special events. Traditional etiquette demands that ladies wear corsages with the flowers pointing downwards and gentlemen wear buttonholes with the flowers upright.

ABOVE: *Present buttonholes and corsages in tiny boxes protected by coloured tissue paper, to help them keep fresh until they are worn.*

GENTLEMAN'S BUTTONHOLE

MATERIALS
1 stem 'Ecstasy' rose
scissors
medium-gauge florist's wire
florist's tape
3 heads eryngium (sea holly)
3 heads lavender
2 ivy leaves

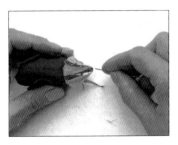

1 Assemble all the ingredients. Cut the stem off the rose about 1 cm (½ in) below the head. Push a small piece of florist's wire through the remaining stem up into the head. Check that the wire feels quite secure and not likely to become loose.

2 Pull the florist's tape so that it stretches and bind it around the stem and wire, sealing them together. Repeat this step, wiring and taping the eryngium stems and the lavender, to create two little bunches.

3 Wire the ivy leaves (see Lady's Corsage). Then arrange one individual flower with the ivy leaves so that the leaves form a flat back to the buttonhole. Ensure that the wires are completely covered.

4 To make the ivy leaves more stable, create a loop of wire at the back of the buttonhole to support each leaf.

LADY'S CORSAGE

MATERIALS
medium-gauge florist's wire
2 stems 'First Red' roses
fine silver reel wire
2 large ivy leaves and 1 smaller one
florist's tape
2 sprigs cotoneaster berries
co-ordinating ribbon, preferably wired

1 Wire the roses. Thread the fine wire through the main vein on each ivy leaf, leaving one long end.

2 Wrap the shorter wire around the stem. Wind the longer wire around the stem and other wire. Tape.

3 Add the roses and berries. Bind the stems and tie with a ribbon.

ROSE POTPOURRIS

In times when personal hygiene did not exist and rubbish and worse were thrown from the most convenient window, scented flowers and plants were essential to disguise the vile odours encountered in everyday life. Dried herbs were burned in fireplaces to stave off the dreaded plague and floors were covered with branches of fragrant lavender, rosemary, sage and other aromatic "strewing" herbs. Bowls were filled with dried scented roses to sweeten the air.

The name "potpourri" means, literally, "rot-pot", and the moist method of making the mixture involves mushing together petals and spices with salt and sometimes brandy and leaving in a jar for a week. The dry method is simpler and the results look more attractive. To make quantities of potpourri, you need to grow – as well as roses – lavender, scented pelargonium (geranium), dianthus (garden pinks) and other brightly coloured flowers.

Orris root is required in both moist and dry potpourri recipes. This is a powdered root which acts as a fixative in these scented blends and is available from traditional pharmacists and herbalists.

Lay freshly picked rose petals and leaves on blotting paper or other absorbent paper, making sure that the petals are not touching. Leave to dry in a cool place where there is a good flow of air. Sprays of flowers like delphiniums need to have their individual flower-heads removed from the stem. Use only when the petals are completely dry.

ROSE AND DELPHINIUM POTPOURRI

MATERIALS
250 g (9 oz) dried scented rose petals
90 g (3½ oz) dried delphinium
flowers and marigold petals
large screw-topped jar
15 ml (1 tbsp) dried mint leaves
5 ml (1 tsp) ground cloves
5 ml (1 tsp) ground cinnamon
5 ml (1 tsp) ground allspice
15 ml (1 tbsp) ground orris root
8 drops rose essential oil

1 Mix the petals and flowers together in the jar, adding the other ingredients one by one. Shake well in between each addition. Screw the lid on tightly and leave for two or three days in a dark cupboard.

ABOVE: *When the petals are completely dry, they are ready to be made into potpourri.*

LEFT: *Petals and rose-heads need to be left somewhere cool and dry with a good air flow.*

CITRUS AND ROSE-SCENTED POTPOURRI

MATERIALS
250 g (9 oz) dried scented rose petals
90 g (3½ oz) dried lavender and
lemon balm
airtight container
dried grated peel of 2 large lemons
5 ml (1 tsp) ground allspice
5 ml (1 tsp) ground orris root

1 Mix the flowers and herbs together in an airtight container, add the lemon peel and leave for two to three days. Add the spice and orris root, shake well, and leave for a week, stirring occasionally.

RIGHT: *The aroma of Rose and Delphinium Potpourri can be enhanced by adding a few drops of rose essential oil or rose geranium oil.*

$\mathcal{S}$UMMER POTPOURRI

$\mathcal{T}$he traditional potpourri is based on rose petals. This is because when rose petals are fresh, they have a powerful fragrance. Some of their distinctive fragrance is retained when they are dried, unlike many other perfumed flowers. Today's potpourri does not rely entirely on the fragrance of its flowers, since there is a wide range of scented oils available and this means materials can be used just for their visual qualities.

This potpourri is traditional in that it uses dried roses, but modern in that whole buds and heads have been included, instead of petals. The sea holly heads, apple slices and whole lemons are used entirely for their appearance.

MATERIALS
20 stems lavender
15 slices preserved (dried) apple
5 dried lemons
1 handful cloves
20 heads dried pale pink roses
2 handfuls dried rose-buds
1 handful hibiscus buds
10 eryngium (sea holly) heads
large glass bowl
potpourri essence
tablespoon

RIGHT: *Predominantly pink and purple, the look and scent of this potpourri will enhance your home throughout the summer months.*

1 Break the stems off the lavender leaving only the flower spikes.

Place all the dried ingredients in the glass bowl and mix together thoroughly. Add several drops of potpourri essence to the mixture of materials – the more you add, the stronger the scent. Stir thoroughly with a spoon to mix the scent throughout the potpourri. As the perfume weakens with time it can be topped up by the addition of a few more drops of essence.

HEART AND FLOWERS

A heart-shaped dried-flower decoration with a traditional feel of the country. The construction of the heart could not be simpler and it will last a long time, if you do not hang it in direct sunlight. This is a lovely way to preserve the best of summer's harvest of roses to enjoy throughout the winter months.

MATERIALS

4 long florist's wires
florist's tape (optional)
florist's reel wire
hay
dark green florist's spray paint
clear glue or glue gun
wide red ribbon
narrow gold ribbon
large and small dried red roses
dried hydrangea heads
scissors

2 Using reel wire, bind hay all the way around the heart, to create a firm frame about twice the thickness of a pencil. Work around the heart at least twice with the reel wire, trapping as many loose ends of hay as possible. Cut off and tie the wire, and trim any loose ends of hay. Spray the whole frame dark green and leave it to dry.

3 Glue the end of the red ribbon to the bottom of the heart and wrap it around the frame. Repeat with the gold ribbon. Tie a bow at the top with a length of gold ribbon. Cut any stems from the roses and separate the hydrangea into florets. Glue the large rose-heads near the centre and surround them with hydrangea. Put the smaller rose-heads along the top.

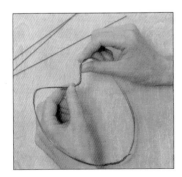

1 Form two pairs of florist's wires into a heart shape. The double thickness of the wire gives the arrangement better support. Tape or twist the ends together at the top and bottom of the heart.

ABOVE: *Roses are a symbol of romance* par excellence *and so what better way to preserve some beautiful garden roses than to combine them with that other emblem of romance: the heart.*

Starfish and Rose Table Decoration

This is an original decoration for a large church candle, using dried rose-heads and starfish. The result is a table-centre decoration with a seaside feel. This is a simple and quick decoration to make, but is very effective nonetheless.

WARNING: Never leave burning candles unattended.

MATERIALS
9 small dried starfish
florist's wires
church candle, 13 x 23 cm (5 x 9 in)
13 cm (5 in) ring plastic foam for
*   dried flowers*
scissors
reindeer moss
40 heads dried roses

1 Double-leg mount all the starfish individually through one arm with florist's wires, to extend their overall length. Cut the wires to approximately 2.5 cm (1 in) in length and put the starfish to one side.

2 Position the candle in the centre of the plastic foam ring. Make 4.5 cm (1¾ in) long hairpins from cut lengths of florist's wires. Use these to pin the reindeer moss around the edge of the ring.

ABOVE: The cream roses complement the colour of the candle and contrast is provided by the apricot colour and strong geometric shape of the small dried starfish.

OPPOSITE: Make sure that you replace the candle well before it reaches the level of the roses.

3 Group the wired starfish into sets of three and position each group equidistant from the others around the foam ring. Push their wires into the foam to secure.

4 Cut the stems of the dried rose-heads to about 2.5 cm (1 in) and push the stems into the foam to form two continuous, tightly packed rings of flowers around the candle.

CHRISTMAS CENTREPIECE

Even the humblest materials can be put together to make an elegant centrepiece. The garden shed has been raided for this one, which is made from a terracotta flowerpot and wire mesh. Fill it up with red berries, ivies and white roses for a rich, Christmassy look; or substitute seasonal flowers and foliage at any other time of the year.

MATERIALS
knife
1 block plastic foam
18 cm (7 in) terracotta pot
about 1 m (39 in) wire mesh
beeswax candle
tree ivy
white roses
red berries
variegated trailing ivy

1 Cut the plastic foam to fit in the terracotta pot and soak it in water. Push the foam in the pot.

Place the pot in the centre of a square of wire mesh. Bring the mesh up around the pot and bend it into position. Position the candle carefully in the centre of the pot. Arrange tree-ivy leaves around the candle.

2 Add a white rose as a focal point, and arrange bunches of red berries among the ivy. Add more white roses, and intersperse trailing variegated ivy among the tree ivy.

WARNING: Never leave burning candles unattended.

OPPOSITE: *The wire mesh gives a strong, curving shape that is nevertheless light and airy. Its ruggedness prevents the traditional Christmassy elements from seeming clichéd.*

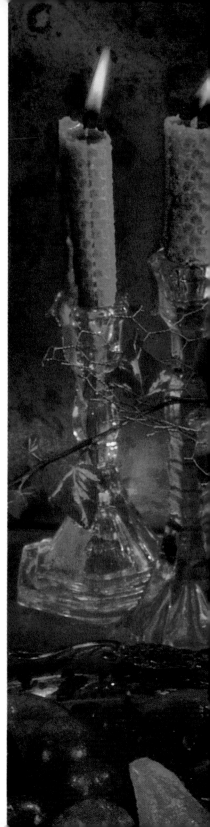

CANDLE POT WITH PERFUMED ROSES

This is a delicate and appealing design, based on a flower-filled hay collar that is secured to the top of a pot, leaving the centre free for a large candle. You could make one for each table setting at a dinner party; or, alternatively, make a few larger pots as a centrepiece, with vibrant green moss and small fruits arranged around their bases.

WARNING: Never leave burning candles unattended.

MATERIALS
large handful of hay
florist's reel wire
scissors
terracotta pot
strong, clear glue or glue gun
moss
dried rose-heads
small-leaved dried foliage, such as
    bupleurum
candle

OPPOSITE: In these delightful candle pots, one shows a simple combination of pink roses and bupleurum, while the other is a mixture of large and miniature roses. With this version, add the smaller roses after filling the main gaps with bupleurum. Perfumed oil gives a wonderful lasting fragrance to the display; sprinkle a few drops of rose oil on the moss.

1 Make the hay collar by scrunching the hay up into a sausage. Wind reel wire around it tightly at 1 cm (½ in) intervals. Measure around the inside rim of the pot before trimming its length to fit.

2 Glue the hay collar into place, so that it is stuck inside the rim of the pot as near to the top as possible. Hold it firmly in position for a few seconds, while the glue begins to harden.

3 Glue moss to the collar, so that it also covers the rim of the pot. Now you are ready to start adding flowers. Carefully cut the rose-heads from their stems, and start to glue them into position.

4 Work from one side of the pot to the other so that you keep the flowers balanced. Make sure that the hole in the centre of the pot remains large enough to take the candle. After the roses, fill any gaps with greenery. Next, place moss in the base so that it half fills the pot. Press it down firmly to form a solid base for the candle. The aim is to have as much of the candle exposed as possible.

SUMMER CANDLE-CUFF

Choose a tall, wide candle for this project, so that the cuff is large enough to apply the dried-flower materials. The candle must be at least twice the height of the cuff, so that it has plenty of room to burn without any danger of setting the hessian alight. Make sure the candle is well wrapped before the start of the project, to ensure that it is kept clean and that the hot glue will not melt the wax as it is applied to the paper base and hessian.

WARNING: Never leave burning candles unattended.

MATERIALS
scissors
thick brown paper
candle
adhesive tape
hessian
strong, clear glue or glue gun
rope
twigs
florist's wire
green moss
6 stems dried roses

1 Cut a piece of brown paper approximately 8 cm (3¼ in) wide and long enough to wrap around your chosen candle. Tape the loose end down; you must be able to move the paper collar freely up and down the candle.

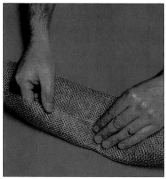

2 Cut a piece of hessian twice as wide as the paper and long enough to wrap around the candle. Fold in the two outside quarters to meet in the middle and glue them down.

3 Lay the candle on the wrong side of the fabric and apply a little glue on either side of the candle. Wrap the fabric tightly around the candle, smoothing it to fit the paper neatly, and applying additional glue where necessary.

4 Trim the corners of the exposed edge and glue them down with a small dab of glue.

5 Wrap the rope around the hessian cuff once and hold it in place. Apply glue all the way around the rope, so that the glue comes into contact with both the rope and the hessian. Wrap the rope around the candle again, as close as possible to the first wrap, pushing it into the hot glue. Repeat the process until the whole of the cuff has been covered.

6 Make a small bundle of twigs and centre-wire it. Glue the bundle and some green moss to the cuff at an angle, using the moss to cover the wire that holds the twigs together. Cut the heads from the roses and glue them around the twigs.

RIGHT: This project requires a little patience but, when you have mastered the technique, you can vary it by using different materials, such as fir cones, dried mushrooms and dried white roses for a wintry look.

DRIED ROSE POMANDER

A pomander is generally defined as a ball of mixed aromatic substances. However, this pomander is designed more for its visual impact than its scent. It would look particularly attractive if carried by a bridesmaid, and a young child might find this easier to manage than a posy. Alternatively it can be hung in the bedroom, perhaps on the dressing-table.

MATERIALS

scissors
10 stems glycerined eucalyptus
15 cm (6 in) ball plastic foam for
*   dried flowers*
3.5 cm (1⅜ in) wide ribbon
florist's wires
30 stems dried pink roses
florist's tape
12 stems dried pale pink peonies
12 preserved (dried) apple slices
1 dried ti tree

1 Cut the eucalyptus stems into approximately 10 cm (4 in) lengths. Take care to ensure that the stem ends are clean and sharp, and carefully push them into the plastic foam, distributing them evenly over its surface.

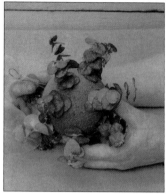

2 Cut a length of ribbon long enough to make a looped carrying handle. Make a loop in the ribbon and double-leg mount the two cut ends together on florist's wire. Push the wire firmly into the plastic foam ball, to form the carrying handle.

3 Cut the stems of the dried roses to approximately 4 cm (1½ in) and wire individually with florist's wire. Group together in threes, bind with wire and cover with tape. Cut the dried peony stems to approximately 4 cm (1½ in) and wire them individually, then tape the stems. Finally, wire the dried apple slices individually on florist's wires.

4 Push the wired peonies into the plastic foam, distributing them evenly all over the ball. Push the wired apple slices into the foam, also distributing them evenly over the ball.

5 Push the ten groups of wired roses into the foam, distributing them evenly all over. Cut the ti tree stems into 9 cm (3½ in) lengths and push into the foam to fill any gaps around the ball. Once completed, you may wish gently to reposition individual elements, in order to achieve the most pleasing effect.

ABOVE: This charming scented ball can be used as a bridesmaid's bouquet or hung in a bedroom.

ROSE AND CLOVE POMANDER

This pomander is a decadent display of rose-heads massed in a ball. But it has a secret: cloves hidden between the rose-heads give the pomander a lasting spicy perfume.

Its dramatic impact relies on the use of large quantities of tightly packed flowers, which should all be of the same type and colour.

MATERIALS
ribbon, 40 x 2.5 cm (16 x 1 in)
florist's wires
10 cm (4 in) ball plastic foam for
   dried flowers
scissors
100 stems dried roses
200 cloves

ABOVE: Almost profligate in its use of materials, this pomander is quick to make and would be a wonderful and very special gift.

1 Fold the ribbon in half and double-leg mount its cut ends together with a florist's wire. To form a ribbon handle, push the wires right through the plastic foam ball so that they come out of the other side, and pull the projecting wires so that the double-leg-mounted part of the ribbon is firmly embedded in the plastic foam. Turn the excess wire back into the foam.

2 (Left) Cut the stems of the roses to approximately 2.5 cm (1 in). Push the stems into the foam, to form a tightly packed circle around the base of the ribbon handle. Push a clove between each rose-head. Continue forming circles of rose-heads and cloves until the foam ball is completely covered.

ROSE-BUD AND CARDAMOM POMANDER

These rose-bud pomanders are fun to make and add a pretty touch to any room. They can be hung on a wall, or over a dressing-table mirror. When the colour has faded they can be sprayed gold to make an effective Christmas ornament.

MATERIALS
ribbon or cord for hanging
medium florist's wires
7.5 cm (3 in) ball plastic foam for
    dried flowers
scissors
small rose-buds
all-purpose glue
green cardamom pods

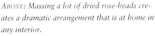

ABOVE: Massing a lot of dried rose-heads creates a dramatic arrangement that is at home in any interior.

1 Make a long loop with the ribbon or cord. Bind the base of the loop with wire. Leave a long end of wire, and push this through the centre of the ball and out through the other side. Trim the wire to about 2.5 cm (1 in) long, and bend the end over so that it is lost in the foam ball.

2 Stick the rose-buds into the foam by their stems. If they have no stems, use a little glue. Cover the entire ball with roses, pressing them close together to make sure that none of the foam is visible. Once the ball is completely covered, glue some green cardamom pods between the rose-buds, to give a contrast in colour and texture.

ABOVE: Roses look delightful when used in topiary balls, but take great care when handling the flowers as the petals tend to crumble easily. When you first start to work on a ball, cut all the stems to the same length before you begin, so that it will be easier for you to achieve a perfect round shape. As you work, trim the stems and adjust the flowers so that they are all at the same height.

ROSE-SCENTED BAGS

A translucent, gossamer fabric made into a simple bag and filled with scented rose-heads and petals is a delightfully feminine idea for a guest room. Keep the flowers lightly perfumed, by adding a few drops from a small bottle of pot-pourri refresher. Larger bags with a drawstring hung in a wardrobe will emit a faint but pleasant aroma each time the door is opened. You could make an alternative to a Christmas stocking by filling a large version with dried rose petals and tiny gifts. Choose fabric that is either extremely fine or transparent, such as organza, fine silk and chiffon, or open-weave linen or muslin, which will allow the perfumed flowers to breathe through it.

MATERIALS
outer fabric, 35 x 24 cm (14 x 9½ in)
lining fabric, 35 x 24 cm (14 x 9½ in)
dressmaker's pins
needle and matching thread
dressmaker's scissors
iron
length of co-ordinating cord, about
   40 cm (16 in)
adhesive tape
2 matching tassels
dried scented rose petals

1 Lay the outer and lining fabrics one on top of the other, right sides together. Sew a seam around all four sides, leaving a 3 cm (1¼ in) gap on one side. Turn the bag through this gap, so that it is right-side out. Press all four seams and slip-stitch the small gap closed. About one-quarter of the way down the bag, run two lines of stitches across the width of the bag, about 2 cm (¾ in) apart. This is to accommodate the drawstring.

Fold the bag in half, with the right sides together. Sew up the bottom and side of the bag. Turn right-sides out and press.

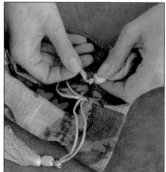

2 At the side seam, make a small snip in the outer fabric, to allow the drawstring through. Take care not to cut through both layers of fabric.

Wind a piece of adhesive tape around the end of the cord, to prevent it from fraying, and feed it into the gap in the seam. Feed it all the way around the bag until it comes out at the other side through another small hole. Tie a single loop in both ends of the cord and attach a matching tassel to the end of each cord.

3 Fill the bag with scented rose petals. Pull the cord, to create gathers in the neck of the bag. Tie a knot to secure the bag and neaten any edges.

OPPOSITE: *A few drops of rose essential oil will refresh the petals and keep the rose bags lovely and fragrant.*

ROSE AND LAVENDER-SCENTED SACHETS

Scented cushions are a charming way to scent your home. They release their fragrance every time they are leaned against.

ROSE AND LAVENDER-SCENTED SACHETS

MATERIALS

50 g (2 oz) rose petals and buds
10 g (¼ oz) lavender flowers
10 g (¼ oz) oakmoss (optional)
5 bay leaves, crumbled
15 ml (1 tbsp) ground cinnamon
15 ml (1 tbsp) ground orris root
10 drops rose oil
40 cm (16 in) square muslin
needle and matching thread
30 x 60 cm (12 x 24 in) thick wadding
30 cm (12 in) square cushion cover

1 Mix all the dry ingredients in a bowl and add the rose oil.

2 Fold the muslin in half twice and seam along two sides to create a bag 20 cm (8 in) square. Fill with the aromatic mixture and stitch the opening closed.

3 (Left) Place the scented bag on the wadding and fold the wadding over the bag. Stitch around the wadding to create the pad for the cushion. Slip the scented cushion pad into the cover.

ROSE-SCENTED SACHETS

Make the sachets in the same way as Rose and Lavender-scented Sachets and then fill with the following:

MATERIALS

75 g (3 oz) scented red rose petals
25 g (1 oz) ground orris root
25 drops rose oil

LEFT: *Scented sachets are a simple, yet delight-ful gift to receive.*

OPPOSITE: *A scented cushion tucked in amongst the others on a sofa will release its delicate fragrance when it is leaned against.*

Scented Rose Cushion

Making this cushion could not be simpler – it requires no sewing at all, just a safety pin! The lace is fine enough to allow the rose scent to permeate into a clothes drawer or through a pile of pillows on a bed. Every now and then, a small amount of essential oil or pot-pourri refreshing perfume will be needed to refresh the petals. Tiny sachets can also be made from circles of the thinnest muslin or by using lace handkerchiefs.

Make a small pile of potpourri in the centre of the fabric, crushing or tearing some of the larger petals or rose-heads. Gather the fabric together and tie it securely with a fine ribbon. Small silk or fabric rose-buds or flowers can then be sewn or glued on to decorate the neck of the bag.

If you are giving a present of fine linen or lingerie, the addition of two or three rose sachets makes more of your gift.

Materials
lace or fine synthetic lace curtain
*   fabric, 25 cm (10 in) square*
pins
scissors
90 cm (1 yard) two colours of thin
*   silk ribbon*
safety pin
rose-scented potpourri

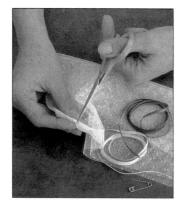

1 Fold the fabric in half and pin the edges together. Make small cuts through both pieces of fabric 2 cm (¾ in) from the edge and at small intervals all the way round.

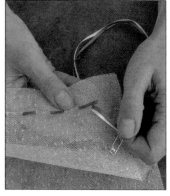

2 Attaching one end of both pieces of ribbon to the safety pin, thread it through the holes, leaving a small gap on one side of the cushion for filling with potpourri.

3 Fill the cushion with rose-scented potpourri through the small opening. Crush or tear the larger petals or rose-heads to fit through the small opening.

4 When the cushion is filled, continue threading the ribbon to close the gap and tie in a bow. If you pull the ribbon tight, you can give the hem a ruched effect.

OPPOSITE: *Scented sachets can be made from lace handkerchiefs that are simply tied up with a piece of ribbon.*

ROSE HAIR SLIDE

Long-lasting and resilient hair slides and bands made with fabric roses are ideal for tiny bridesmaids who cannot resist putting their hands in their hair every few minutes, reserving the fresh flowers for posies or small baskets.

MATERIALS
glue gun with all-purpose glue
*   sticks*
metal hair slide
fabric roses with leaves

ABOVE: *There are some striking silk and taffeta roses available in muted colours.*

1 Always take great care with glue guns as the glue is very hot. Insert the glue stick and wait for the gun to heat up. The trigger will pull easily when the glue has melted.

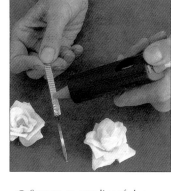

2 Squeeze an even line of glue along the top edge of the hair slide, always keeping your fingers well clear of the piping hot glue.

3 Stick the rose-heads to the slide pointing to alternate sides, so that their bases are completely covered.

4 Turn the slide over and add more glue to stick fabric leaves to the slide, to fill any gaps that remain.

$\mathcal{S}$TEMMED TARTAN ROSES

$\mathcal{W}$hat would every gardener not give to have produced roses of such wondrous colours and lasting beauty? Fun to make and certain to be a talking point, these tartan roses can be adapted to suit many occasions. Make them the centrepiece of a festive table or use them to decorate place settings. Alternatively, you can make them part of a festive wreath or garland, or stitch a single tartan rose to a plain evening dress or evening bag.

MATERIALS
florist's wire, 20 cm (8 in)
tartan ribbon, 60 cm x 4 cm
    (24 x 1½ in)
needle and matching thread
scissors
tartan wire-edged ribbon, 30 cm x
    4 cm (12 x 1½ in)
fine florist's wire
florist's tape

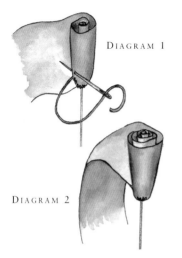

DIAGRAM 1

DIAGRAM 2

1 Bend the end of a piece of stub wire to form a hook equal in depth to the ribbon width. Holding the tartan ribbon with the cut end to the right, hook the wire through the upper right-hand corner of the ribbon, approximately 5 mm (¼ in) from the edge. Close the hook to hold the ribbon.

2 Roll the ribbon around the hook two or three times from right to left, to enclose the wire. Stitch to secure *(see diagram 1)*. Then, holding the wire stem in your right hand and the loose ribbon in your left, fold the ribbon so that it runs down parallel to the wire *(see diagram 2)*.

3 Roll the covered hook end from right to left into the fold, turning tightly at the bottom and loosely at the top until the ribbon is once again horizontal to the wire.

4 With the wire stem facing towards you, stitch the base of the rose to secure it in place.

5 Continue folding the ribbon and rolling the rose in this way, stitching the base after each fold until the desired shape and size of rose are achieved. To complete the rose, cut the ribbon squarely, fold it back neatly on to the rose and stitch lightly to hold in place *(see diagram 3)*.

6 To make the triple leaf, cut the wire-edged ribbon into three equal lengths. Cut three equal lengths of fine florist's wire and make a small loop in each about 2.5 cm (1 in) from one end.

7 Fold two corners of a piece of wire-edged ribbon down and forwards to form a triangle. Place one of the pieces of wire centrally in the triangle, with the loop on the lower selvedge and the short wire end pointing upwards. Stitch the ribbon to secure the wire in place.

DIAGRAM 3

8 Fold the lower corners of the ribbon triangle under and backwards to create a leaf shape. Gather the lower part of the leaf neatly round the long wire stem and stitch to secure in place.

9 Make two more leaves in this way. Bind the wire stems of two of the leaves with florist's tape for about 1 cm (½ in). Bind the wire stem of the third leaf for approximately 2.5 cm (1 in). Join the three leaves together at this point and continue binding around all three wires to create a single stem. Bind the stem of the tartan rose, binding in the triple leaf about 10 cm (4 in) down from the rose.

OPPOSITE: *Roses made from tartan ribbon are amusing and cheerful and would make a striking part of a contemporary Christmas table setting.*

ROSE HAIR SLIDE

Ribbon roses are surprisingly straightforward to make and can be used to trim a wide range of gift items and sewing projects. The choice of harmonizing colours in a variety of ribbon widths gives a charming posy effect to this hair accessory, which would be ideal for a young bridesmaid. A fabric-covered hair band could also be decorated with a row of flowers or a straight bar clip could be trimmed with pearls.

MATERIALS

50 x 4 cm (20 x 1½ in) cream lace
10 cm (4 in) oval hair slide
PVA glue
20 cm x 3 mm (8 x ⅛ in) pale green ribbon
20 cm x 3 mm (8 x ⅛ in) each, pale pink, dark rose pink and beige ribbon
For the roses:
needle and matching sewing threads
80 x 2.5 cm (32 x 1 in) warm beige ribbon
75 x 2.5 cm (30 x 1 in) dark rose pink ribbon
50 x 1 cm (20 x ½ in) pale pink ribbon
30 x 1 cm (12 x ½ in) cream ribbon
60 x 5 mm (24 x ¼ in) dark rose pink ribbon
30 x 5 mm (12 x ¼ in) dark pink ribbon

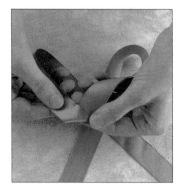

1 To make a ribbon rose, thread a needle with matching thread and have this standing by for the final step. Fold the ribbon at a right angle, two-thirds along its length, and hold in place.

2 Pass the long end under the triangular fold and hold with your other hand. Pass the short end under, then continue to make concertina folds to the end of the ribbon.

3 Hold the two ends together, and gently grip with the thumb and forefinger of one hand. Carefully draw up the long end. This ruffles the ribbon and forms the rose petals.

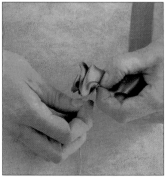

4 Still holding the rose, make several stab stitches, being sure to pass through all the layers of ribbon. Fasten off the thread and trim the ends of the ribbon.

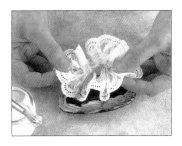

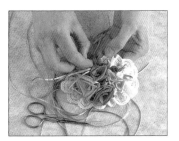

5 Gather the lace along the straight edge and draw up to fit on to the hair slide. Tucking the raw ends neatly under, glue in place with PVA glue and leave to dry.

6 Following the method given, make the roses: one warm beige, two large dark rose pink, three pale pink, two cream, one small dark rose pink, three dark pink. Arrange the roses inside the gathered lace and stick in place, one at a time, with the larger roses towards the centre of the hair slide.

7 Cut several 4 cm (1½ in) lengths of the green ribbon and stitch the ends together to form loops. Sew these between the roses along one outer edge. Make loops and streamers from the rest of the narrow ribbons and attach as shown.

$\mathcal{V}$ELVET ROSE COAT HANGER

$\mathcal{P}$erfect for hanging up a special garment or to give as a gift, this coat hanger makes use of the luxurious texture and rich colours of velvet to recreate the charm of roses in full bloom. Ready-made fabric leaves are easily available.

MATERIALS
tape measure
wadding
dressmaking scissors
wooden coat hanger
needle and matching sewing threads
paper
pencil
green and red velvet
sewing machine
fabric leaves
matching narrow velvet ribbon

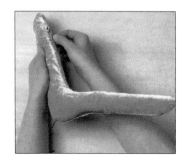

1 Cut two pieces of wadding about 30 cm (12 in) square. Wrap each arm of the hanger in wadding and sew it in place. To make the paper template, put the hanger on a sheet of paper and draw around it. Add 1.5 cm (⅝ in) all around and around the ends. Cut two pieces of green velvet to this size. With right sides together, stitch the upper edge and the rounded ends.

2 Turn right-sides out. Unpick the centre and slip the velvet over the hanger. Slip-stitch the bottom edges together.

3 Cut a piece of red velvet 10 x 30 cm (4 x 12 in), fold it in half lengthways and stitch the long edge and one short edge. Turn right-sides out. Roll up the velvet from the unstitched short end, to make a rose, and secure it with a prick stitch.

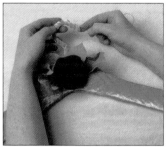

4 Stitch the rose and fabric leaves to the hanger. Wrap the ribbon around the hook and slip-stitch.

LEFT: *For your most special and treasured clothes, a decorative padded hanger will not only protect delicate fabrics but also add to the excitement of dressing up.*

RIBBONWORK CHRISTENING PILLOW

Create an heirloom gift combining the freshness of pure white cotton with the silky-soft appeal of roses and other flowers embroidered in delicate pastels. Duplicate the embroidery design on a cot quilt for a pretty but practical duo that will see service for many years. This type of ribbon embroidery is easy to work and can produce lifelike effects.

MATERIALS

tape measure

white cotton piqué, 90 x 30 cm
    (36 x 12 in)

scissors

lightweight iron-on interfacing,
    23 x 23 cm (9 x 9 in)

iron

dressmaker's carbon or vanishing
    marker pen

embroidery hoop

chenille needle

satin ribbon in pale pink, mid pink,
    dusky pink, pale mint green,
    pale lime green, pale aqua,
    1.75 m x 3 mm (2 yd x ⅛ in) of
    each

ribbon, 1.4 m x 5 mm (1½ yd x ¼ in)

narrow broderie anglaise insertion,
    1.4 m (1½ yd)

broderie anglaise edging,
    1.4 m x 7.5 cm (1½ yd x 3 in)

dressmaker's pins

needle and matching and contrasting
    threads

tapestry needle

cushion pad, 30 x 30 cm (12 x 12 in)

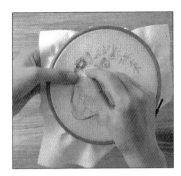

1 Cut a 23 x 23 cm (9 x 9 in) square of cotton piqué and iron the interfacing to one side. Transfer the garland design to the fabric, by tracing it through dressmaker's carbon or by drawing it freehand with a vanishing marker pen. Mount the fabric in an embroidery hoop. Work the roses, by stitching a star shape of four overlapping straight stitches in pale pink. With darker pink ribbon, work a circle of overlapping, slightly longer stitches around the centre to make the effect of petals.

2 Using the various shades of green ribbon, work the leaves in straight stitch and the rose-buds in lazy daisy stitch. Work a single pink straight stitch for the centre of each rose-bud and fill any spaces with small French knots. Work the rest of the garland design using a range of formal and random stitches. The photograph will act as a guide. Trim the finished piece to a 15 cm (6 in) square. Finish with a small, single-loop bow made from a piece of 5 mm (¼ in) ribbon.

3 (Left) Cut four 9 cm (3½ in) squares of cotton piqué. Cut four 15 x 9 cm (6 x 3½ in) rectangles. Cut the broderie anglaise insertion in four 9 cm (3½ in), two 15 cm (6 in) and two 33 cm (13 in) lengths. Edge one side of each square and one long side of two of the rectangles using a 1 cm (½ in) seam allowance. Sew the insertion-edged rectangles to opposite sides of the embroidered square. Sew an insertion-edged square to either end of the two remaining rectangles.

4 Use the two remaining strips of broderie anglaise insertion to join all three strips together, thus framing the embroidered square (see diagram 1). Press the seam allowance towards the central square on the wrong side.

T E M P L A T E

5 Join the two ends of the broderie anglaise edging and run a gathering thread along the raw edge. Fold the edging into four equal sections, marking each quarter division with a small scissor cut. Pin each of these cuts to one corner of the pillow top, on the right side. Draw up the gathering thread to fit the cushion. Distribute the gathers evenly, allowing a little extra fullness at the corners. Pin the broderie anglaise around the outside edge so that it lies on top of the cushion. Tack and then sew in place.

6 Thread the 5 mm (¼ in) ribbon through the insertion using the tapestry needle, securing each end with a few tacking stitches.

7 (Right) Cut a 30 cm (12 in) square of cotton piqué for the pillow back. Pin to the right side of the pillow front, ensuring that the lace is free of the seam line. Sew around three sides then turn to the right side. Insert the cushion pad and slip-stitch the fourth side closed.

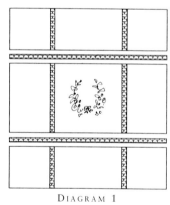

D I A G R A M   1

OPPOSITE: *Ribbonwork roses combine with cotton piqué and broderie anglaise to make this exquisite pillow. It will be treasured for years.*

SATIN-ROSE HAT DECORATION

Decorate a straw hat for a summer wedding or garden party with a vibrant rose made of satin ribbon. Use ribbons of different widths and colours to make a bunch of roses or stick to one beautiful specimen that will catch every eye.

MATERIALS
scissors
satin ribbon in 3 complementary
  shades
needle and matching sewing threads
green florist's wires
green ribbon
green crêpe paper or florist's tape

RIGHT: *Satin ribbon has all the lustre of real rose petals and a satin rose will give a plain and simple straw hat all the promise of summer but will last unfaded into the depths of winter.*

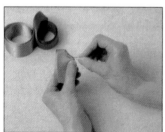

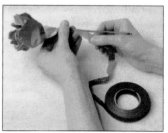

1 Make each petal separately, starting with the centre petal. Cut a piece of ribbon, about twice the width of the ribbon in length, and fold it with wrong sides together. Fold over each of the top corners twice and stitch them down invisibly. Repeat to make enough petals for a rose, using different shades and widths of ribbon.

2 Roll the centre petal around itself and secure with a stitch. Insert a stem wire into this first petal and continue to add petals around the rose, stitching them together as you go.

3 Finish the rose by binding with green ribbon, to hide the raw edges. Stitch it in place at the top, just over the base of the petals, and then gather up the lower edge neatly and stitch it securely. Bind the stem with crêpe paper or florist's tape.

OPPOSITE: *Beautiful blowsy paper roses grace a simple straw hat, turning it into something to wear for a special occasion.*

RIBBON-ROSE HAIR BAND

Choose ribbons to match a bridesmaid's outfit or a party dress. With practice, these pretty ribbon roses will be easy to make.

MATERIALS

60 cm (24 in) length of 6 cm (2¼ in) tartan ribbon

needle and matching sewing thread

scissors

2 m (2 yd) of 4 cm (1½ in) sheer green plain and gold-edged ribbons

satin-covered padded hair band

38 cm (15 in) lengths of 4 cm (1½ in) gauze and satin ribbons

2 Cut the green ribbon into 15 cm (6 in) lengths and fold them to make leaves. Sew them to the centre of the hair band and then attach the rose in the middle.

3 Make six more roses in different colours and sew them along the hair band, interspersing them with more green leaves in plain and gold-edged ribbon.

1 Make the central rose first. Fold one end of tartan ribbon at a right angle and twist it around twice, to form the centre. Secure at the bottom with a few stitches. Form the first petal by twisting the ribbon around the centre, folding it back at a right angle, so that the top edge lies across the "stalk", and catching it down with a secure stitch. Continue to wrap the ribbon around in this way, securing each petal with a stitch. Finish off firmly, by stitching through all the layers of ribbon.

ABOVE: *Ribbon roses have the advantage that you can make them in almost any colour or pattern, to suit any outfit, and they will last for a long time.*

TUDOR ROSE CUSHION

ABOVE: *The deep, glossy red of real rose petals is reflected in the silk of this cushion, which is quilted with the most classic and traditional rose motif: the Tudor rose.*

The classic Tudor rose motif is picked out in quilting lines on this vibrant silk cushion; the traditional rosy red colour is a perfect complement for the motif.

MATERIALS

tracing paper
pencil
fine black felt-tipped pen
tape measure
red silk taffeta, 100 x 90 cm (40 x 36 in)
quilter's pencil
calico, 100 x 90 cm (40 x 36 in)
dressmaker's scissors
wadding, 50 cm (20 in) square
dressmaker's pins
needle and tacking thread
sewing machine
red sewing thread
vanishing marker pen
piping cord, 1.5 m (1½ yd)
polyester stuffing

1 Trace the Tudor rose template, enlarging it as necessary. Outline the rose in black pen. Cut a 50 cm (20 in) square of silk. Lay the silk on top and trace the rose directly on to the fabric, with the quilter's pencil. Cut a 50 cm (20 in) square of calico. Layer the wadding between the calico and the silk. Tack the layers together with lines of stitches radiating from the centre. Using red thread, quilt along the outlines of the design, working from the centre out. Once complete, draw a five-sided shape around the design and trim the cushion along the lines.

2 Cut and join several 5 cm (2 in) bias strips of red silk. Press the seams open and trim them. Fold the bias strip over the piping cord and tack. Pin and tack the piping around the edge of the cushion, with the raw edges together. Machine-stitch close to the piping. Lay a square of silk and then of calico over the right side of the cushion. Pin, tack and stitch around the edges, leaving a small gap. Trim the seams and corners and turn through. Fill with polyester stuffing and slip-stitch the gap closed.

TWO-TONE ROSE SCARF

Wrap yourself in garlands of roses by stamping a silk scarf with this red and green rose pattern. Scarves are wonderfully versatile and they really can make an everyday outfit look very special – wear this one around your neck or as a sash, or you could even use it to wrap up your hair, gypsy-style. When you are not wearing your scarf, drape it over a chair or hang it on a peg, to add dashes of colour to a room.

The scarf shown here was originally cream but it was then dipped in pink dye for an attractive two-tone effect – a light-coloured scarf would work just as well.

MATERIALS
red and green fabric paint
plates
foam rollers
small rose and rose-bud stamps
silk scarf
backing paper (thin card or newspaper)

ABOVE: *Stamping produces a charmingly informal effect reminiscent of folk art techniques. This rose stamp is perfectly in tune with that informality and will cheer you just by hanging in the room!*

1 Spread the paints on the plates and run the rollers through them until evenly coated. Ink the small rose red and its leaves and the rose-bud stamp green. Stamp them on the corner and edges of the paper.

2 Slip the paper pattern under the scarf and print alternating small roses and rose-buds around the border, using the roses on the backing paper as a positioning guide.

3 Fill the middle of the scarf with two parallel rows of small roses.

BLACK ROSE VASE

The transparency of this plain glass vase creates the illusion that the black rose is floating in mid-air, somewhere above the mantelpiece. Glass is an interesting surface to stamp on because of its smoothness. The paint disperses as soon as it is applied to the glass. Have a spare piece of glass handy, so that you can practise your stamping before committing yourself to the final print. This way, you can find out exactly how much paint you need to get the desired effect.

There are now paints available called acrylic enamels. They are suitable for use on glass and ceramics and give a hard-wearing finish that stands up to non-abrasive washing.

MATERIALS
plain rectangular glass vase
kitchen cloth
black acrylic enamel paint
plate
foam roller
large rose stamp
piece of glass

1 Wash the vase, to remove any grease from the surface. Dry it thoroughly.

2 Spread some black paint on to the plate and run the roller through it, until it is evenly coated. Ink the stamp and make a test print on the glass.

3 Stamp the black rose in the centre of the vase front. Apply gentle pressure with a steady hand and remove the stamp directly, to prevent it from sliding on the slippery surface. If you are not happy with the print, wipe it off before it begins to dry, clean the glass and try again.

ABOVE: *This stamped black rose is graphic and dramatic and, used on a plain vase, would be suitable for the most modern interior.*

ART NOUVEAU ROSE BOX

Inspired by the early-20th century work of the Glasgow School of Art, this design for a simple wooden box combines swirling *art nouveau* shapes and stained-glass style roses to dramatic effect.

MATERIALS
fine-grade sandpaper
white primer paint
oval wooden craft box, with lid
soft pencil
tracing paper
thick bristle and fine hair
*   paintbrushes*
paint-mixing container
rose pink, green, yellow, white, black
*   and blue acrylic paints*
clear acrylic or crackle varnish

ABOVE: This box decorated with roses is the perfect place to keep rose-scented potpourri.

1 Sand and prime the box. Enlarge the template and transfer it to the lid, with a pencil and tracing paper.

2 Paint the rose petals and the leaves as solid blocks of colour.

3 Paint the stems and thorn ring; add shade to the flowers. Paint the leaf veins and outline the petals.

4 Colour-wash the rim of the lid with watered-down rose paint. Paint the box blue. Seal with varnish.

ROSE-STAMPED STATIONERY

ABOVE: *Romantic golden roses embellish inexpensive plain stationery and its box to dramatic effect. Whether you give the stationery box as a gift or use the stationery for your special letters, you will delight the recipient.*

*H*and-printed stationery sends its own message, even before you have added your greetings or invitation. This golden rose would be particularly suitable for wedding stationery, making a welcome change from mass-produced cards.

MATERIALS

tracing paper
hard and soft pencils
linoleum square
lino-cutting tools
gold paint
small paint roller
metal ruler

blank stationery, such as deckle-edged notepaper and envelopes
fine paintbrush
glue stick
stationery box
Japanese paper, cut into strips
ribbon

1 Trace the rose motif, enlarging it as necessary. Transfer to the linoleum. Using a narrow-grooved tool, cut out the motif, keeping your free hand behind the blade at all times. With a wide tool, cut away the excess lino. Indicate with an arrow which edge is the top, on the back.

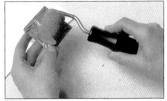

2 Ink the lino stamp with gold paint and stamp the stationery, re-inking the roller each time. Wipe away any build-up of paint.

3 Edge the envelopes, cards and the top edge of the notepaper with a fine line of gold paint. Glue the box with strips of Japanese paper. Arrange the notepaper and cards in the box. Bind the envelopes with more Japanese paper and ribbon and add them to the box. Decorate the box lid with ribbon.

ℛOSE-STENCILLED TABLECLOTH

Two stencils are arranged here to decorate a square tablecloth; the same motifs could be used in many different combinations and scales. Use two or three shades with each stencil shape, to achieve a rounded, three-dimensional look to the roses, leaves and branches.

MATERIALS
tracing paper
hard and soft pencils
stencil card
craft knife
cutting mat
heavy white cotton fabric, 75 cm (30 in) square

spray adhesive
dark pink, pale pink, yellow, dark green, light green and warm brown stencil paints
3 stencil brushes
vanishing marker pen
long ruler
set square
needle and white sewing thread

ABOVE: *Stylized roses and leaves are a charming folk-art motif but, arranged in these dramatic borders, have an unexpected sophistication.*

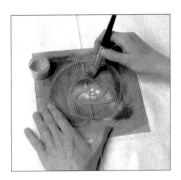

1 Enlarge the rose template so that it measures 15 cm (6 in) across. Enlarge the branch template so that it is 30 cm (12 in) long. Transfer both on to the stencil card and carefully cut out the stencils, with the knife, on the cutting mat.

2 Fold the fabric in half each way, to find the centre. Press lightly along the creases. Spray the back of the rose stencil lightly with adhesive and place it in the middle of the cloth. Start with dark pink paint in the corner petals and round the outer edge of the inner petals.

3 Fill in the rest of the petals with pale pink and colour the centre dots in yellow. Keep the brush upright and use a small circling motion to transfer the paint. Be careful not to overload the bristles. Peel off the stencil and allow the paint to dry.

4 Work a branch motif on each side of the rose, using the crease as a placement guide, to form a cross. Spray the back of the card with adhesive, as before. Stencil yellow paint in the centre of each leaf.

5 Blend dark and light green paints and finish painting the leaves.

6 Work a small amount of brown around the base of the leaves and the outside edge of the branches. Stencil a rose at the end of each branch. With a fabric marker, and using the ruler and set square to get a perfectly accurate square, draw a line about 15 cm (6 in) from each edge, so that it is on the same level as the outer edge of the roses. Stencil a rose in each corner and then work branches between the roses.

7 (Right) When the paint is quite dry, fix it according to the manufacturer's instructions. Turn under, press and stitch a narrow double hem along the outside edge.

Aromatherapy Massage Oil

Rose essential oil is one of the most expensive and is often sold mixed with a small amount of carrier oil such as jojoba. Each essential oil has different qualities and values which a qualified aromatherapist can use to create a specific programme of holistic treatment.

Massage is one of the most effective methods of experiencing the healing properties of these oils. You can create your own massage oil by blending essential oils with a carrier oil such as pure sunflower or grapeseed. Never apply neat essential oil directly on to the skin unless under the supervision of a qualified aromatherapist. Though recommended in many books, it is also unwise to add neat essential oils to a bath as the oil may appear to disperse but will not actually do so and can therefore come in direct contact with the skin, causing an allergic reaction. Essential oils can be immensely beneficial but need to be used advisedly.

Aphrodisiac Massage Oil

A light, non-greasy and fragrant oil for a sensual massage over the entire body which is relaxing and luxurious.

5 drops rose essential oil
3 drops ylang ylang essential oil
2 drops jasmine essential oil
105 ml (7 tbsp) grapeseed oil
5 ml (1 tsp) wheatgerm oil

Harmonious Massage Oil

The essential oils in this blend, combined together, create a harmony related to the ability to love. Rose has healing and sensual qualities; sandalwood is relaxing and sensual; clary sage, euphoric and uplifting; geranium, cleansing and refreshing; ginger, fortifying and warming.

13 drops rose essential oil
2 drops sandalwood essential oil
2 drops clary sage essential oil
3 drops geranium essential oil
3 drops ginger essential oil
20 ml (4 tsp) jojoba oil
105 ml (7 tbsp) unrefined sunflower oil

After Sun Soothing Oil

Prolonged sun-bathing, particularly in the hottest part of the day, can have a devastating effect on the skin. It encourages premature ageing and, if you burn, it can be very painful. Prevention is, of course, better than cure, but if you are feeling tender and, providing the skin is not actually burnt and broken, this massage oil is very comforting and moisturizing.

5 drops rose essential oil
5 drops chamomile essential oil
45 ml (3 tbsp) grapeseed oil
45 ml (3 tbsp) virgin olive oil
15 ml (1 tbsp) wheatgerm oil

1 Mix several essential oils together in a base of carrier oil such as grapeseed, jojoba or sweet almond, to produce a massage oil that has specific therapeutic benefits.

2 Never exceed 1 drop of essential oil for every 20 drops of carrier oil. These oils should be purchased in dropper bottles so it is easy to be accurate when you are making up your own blends.

RIGHT: Rose essential oil is one of the most precious and luxurious of all perfumed flower oils.

FACIAL BEAUTY WITH ROSES

The most delicate skin on the body's surface is on the face and, though true beauty comes from within, there is nothing quite so attractive as a fresh and clear face that radiates good health. Millions are spent each year on beautifying lotions, particularly those reputed to forestall the onset of ageing. Rose essential oil is nourishing and moisturizing and 3–4 drops mixed with 20 ml (4 tsp) jojoba oil make a simple but effective facial oil to apply after the skin has been thoroughly cleansed.

ROSE CREAM CLEANSER AND FACE MASKS

This simple cleanser is mildly astringent with both soothing and cooling properties. It should be made up in small quantities and kept in the refrigerator. If you reduce the rose-water to 5 ml (1 tsp) and replace it with the honey that has been gently warmed, you have a face mask suitable for dry skin but gentle enough for sensitive faces. Adding the oatmeal, stirring well and leaving for 10 minutes produces a mask that can also be used as an exfoliating skin scrub. As with all face masks, this is most effective if used while relaxing in a bath and left on the face and neck for about 10 minutes before washing off very thoroughly.

OPPOSITE: 'Awakening' is a climbing rose with fully double blooms that flower continually through the summer.

MATERIALS
mixing bowl
spoon
105 ml (7 tbsp) triple-distilled rose-water
45 ml (3 tbsp) double cream
30 ml (2 tbsp) unblended clear honey
airtight container
30 ml (2 tbsp) fine-ground oatmeal

1 Mix the rose-water with the cream and honey and stir well. Keep in an airtight container in a cool place until ready to use. To use, smooth over the face and neck.

2 The addition of oatmeal to the honey, cream and rose-water mix makes an exfoliating face mask. Smooth over the face, avoiding eyes and sensitive areas, relax for 10 minutes, then gently rinse off.

ROSE AND CHAMOMILE FACIAL STEAM AND SKIN TONICS

Hot-water facials open the skin's pores and not only make the face feel refreshed but create a sense of well-being and relaxation.

MATERIALS
large bowl
hot water
3 drops rose essential oil
4 drops chamomile essential oil
towel
For the dry skin tonic:
75 ml (5 tbsp) triple-distilled rose-water
30 ml (2 tbsp) orange-flower water
For the oily skin tonic:
90 ml (6 tbsp) triple-distilled rose-water
30 ml (2 tbsp) witch-hazel
airtight bottles

1 Fill a bowl just wider than your face with hot water and add 3 drops rose essential oil and 4 drops chamomile essential oil.

2 Cover your head with a towel and drape it over the bowl. About 5 minutes is usually long enough to feel the benefit. If possible, relax somewhere quiet and dark with subdued lighting for a further 15 minutes.

3 For the skin tonics, combine the ingredients in scrupulously clean bottles and keep cool.

ROSE HAND AND NAIL TREATMENT

To keep hands and nails looking their best, regular use of a good hand cream and a weekly manicure make a noticeable difference. For the two hand oils listed below, mix the ingredients together and store in dark coloured bottles when not in use.

ROSE HAND OIL

Massaging the hands daily keeps the fingers and palms soft and smooth, and the combination of these essential oils is particularly suited to drier and more mature skins. Make sure you massage the backs of the hands to protect against the damaging effects of the sun which can cause liver spots.

MATERIALS
mixing bowl
50 ml/2 fl oz/¼ cup jojoba oil
50 ml/2 fl oz/¼ cup almond oil
6 drops rose essential oil
4 drops sandalwood essential oil
airtight dark bottle

ROSE NAIL OIL

Massaging the base of your nails every day will encourage healthy growth. You can also use this oil as part of a manicure, soaking the nails for at least 10 minutes after you have thoroughly cleaned them.

MATERIALS
mixing bowl
50 ml/2 fl oz/¼ cup almond oil
10 ml (2 tsp) apricot kernel oil
5 drops geranium essential oil
2 drops rose essential oil
airtight dark bottle

ROSE HAND CREAM

This fragrant hand cream is rich in nourishing oils and waxes. Two bowls of thin clear liquids when combined together miraculously produce a thick white mixture.

MATERIALS
50 ml/2 fl oz/¼ cup rose-water
45 ml (3 tbsp) witch-hazel
½ tsp glycerine
¼ tsp borax
saucepan
double boiler
30 ml (2 tbsp) emulsifying wax or
  white beeswax
5 ml (1 tsp) lanolin
30 ml (2 tbsp) almond oil
spoon
2 drops rose essential oil
airtight china or glass pots

1 Gently heat the rose-water, witch-hazel, glycerine and borax in a saucepan until the borax has dissolved. In a double-boiler melt the wax, lanolin and almond oil over a gentle heat.

2 Slowly add the rose-water mixture to the oil mixture, stirring constantly as you do so. It will quickly turn milky and thicken. Remove from the heat and continue to stir while it cools, then add the rose essential oil. Pour the cream into pots and store in a cool place.

OPPOSITE: *'Madame Alfred Carrière' is a beautiful old climbing rose with sweet-smelling creamy-white flowers tinged with blush pink.*

ROSE HAND CREAM FOR WINTER

Richly emollient, this cream is ideal for hands roughened and sore from gardening and other outdoor tasks. It can also be applied as a barrier cream, to prevent soreness in cold weather.

This is a very nourishing cream, incorporating patchouli oil, which is a particularly good healer of cracked and chapped skin. Follow the old country treatment for sore hands by covering them in a generous layer of cream last thing at night and then pulling on a pair of soft cotton gloves. Your hands will have absorbed the cream by morning and feel soft once more. These ingredients make about 475 ml/16 fl oz/2 cups.

MATERIALS
grater
75 g (3 oz) unscented, hard white
    soap
bowl
90 ml (6 tbsp) boiling water
spoon
115 g (4 oz) beeswax
45 ml (3 tbsp) glycerine
150 ml/¼ pint/⅔ cup almond oil
45 ml (3 tbsp) rose-water
double-boiler
whisk
25 drops patchouli oil
glass or china pots and jars

1 Grate the soap and place it in a bowl. Pour over the boiling water and stir together until smooth.

2 Combine the beeswax, glycerine, almond oil and rose-water in a double-boiler. Melt over a gentle heat.

3 Remove from the heat and gradually whisk in the soap mixture. Keep whisking as the mixture cools and thickens. Stir in the patchouli oil, mixing thoroughly, and pour into pots and jars.

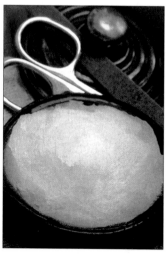

ABOVE: *Winter hand cream with rose water nourishes cracked and chapped hands.*

OPPOSITE: *Hard-working hands will benefit from regular skin care.*

ROSE BATH AND BODY LOTIONS

The Emperor Nero is said to have bathed in pure rose-water and extended this luxury to guests at his frequent banquets, probably contributing to the economic collapse of the Roman Empire! The following simple beauty formulas will not break the bank but are easy to concoct and, when presented in pretty bottles, make lovely gifts.

BELOW: The wonderfully uplifting nature of rose scent makes Rose Body Lotion the perfect accompaniment to any bathtime treat.

ℛose body lotion

This refreshing body lotion keeps well if you pour it into a jar and store it in a cool place.

MATERIALS
mixing bowl
spoon
30 ml (2 tbsp) boiling water
1.5 ml (¼ tsp) borax
5 ml (1 tsp) white beeswax
5 ml (1 tsp) lanolin
30 ml (2 tbsp) petroleum jelly
25 ml (5 tsp) apricot kernel oil
20 ml (4 tsp) unrefined sunflower
   oil
double-boiler
whisk
10 drops rose essential oil
1 drop pink food colouring
tinted glass jar

1 Dissolve the borax in the water. Melt the beeswax, lanolin and petroleum jelly with the apricot kernel and sunflower oils in a double-boiler. Remove from the heat once the wax has melted and stir well. Whisk in the borax solution. Keep whisking until cool. Then add the rose oil and food colouring.

ABOVE: *Use a few drops of the essential oil to give seashells, pebbles and pumice a pleasing aroma.*

ℛose-scented seashells, pebbles and pumice

Collect seashells and pebbles polished smooth from the effect of waves to make this aromatic display.

MATERIALS
seashells
pebbles
pumice
rose-scented room scent or oil

1 Mix the seashells, pebbles and pumice in a bowl. Add a few drops of rose-scented room scent or oil. The slightly porous surfaces will absorb the perfume and create a soft aroma in a room.

LEFT: *Body lotion scented with rose essential oil is luxuriously relaxing and soothing.*

ℒuxurious body scrub

This is a delightful alternative to the loofah, much more gentle and pleasantly aromatic.

MATERIALS
1 tbsp powdered orange rind
3 tbsp ground almonds
1 tbsp oatmeal
90 ml (6 tbsp) almond oil
5 drops rose essential oil
bowl
spoon

1 Simply mix all the ingredients in a bowl when you require it. After a bath, dry yourself thoroughly and rub the mixture into your skin, paying particular attention to dry skin areas. Leave it to dry on the skin and then rub off using a soft flannel.

$\mathcal{R}$OSE-SCENTED TEA AND SUGAR

$\int$cented teas and sugars are simplicity itself but, presented in decorative containers, they are an original gift idea for tea-lovers and keen cooks. Extravagantly wrapped with a box of Festival Shortbreads or Rose-water Biscuits, they make wonderful presents for special festive occasions.

$\mathcal{R}$OSE-SCENTED TEA

The rose petals in this beverage subtly flavour and add a distinctive scent to a high-quality tea such as oolong. This tea, named from the Chinese words *wu* (black), and *lung* (dragon), combines the qualities of black and green teas. The finest blends, known as Formosa oolongs, come from Taiwan and have a rich amber colour and a delicious fruity taste. Pouchong teas are mixed with jasmine and gardenia flowers and you can make your own special blend with rose petals.

INGREDIENTS
200 g (7 oz) highly scented dried rose petals
500 g (1¼ lb) finest quality tea

1 Mix together well in a large bowl and decant into airtight containers, preferably pretty screw-topped jars or decorative tea caddies. Use as any other fine quality tea.

$\mathcal{R}$OSE-SCENTED SUGAR

This delicate sugar has a multitude of uses: it can be used to sweeten cakes and sauces, stirred into cream or yoghurt for a subtle flavouring and substituted for the caster sugar used in Rose-water Biscuits.

INGREDIENTS
20 g/ ¾ oz/5 cups highly scented dried rose petals
250 g/9 oz/1 cup caster sugar

1 Grind the rose petals in a food processor or liquidizer, just until they are the consistency of coarse sand, not a powder. You can use a coffee grinder but first make sure all traces of coffee have been wiped off or its strong flavour will obliterate the rose fragrance.

2 Mix the petals with the sugar and transfer into screw-topped jars or pots. Make sure you use only the finest quality rose petals, which have been thoroughly dried.

LEFT: *These beautifully wrapped Festival Shortbreads would make a lovely gift along with Rose-scented Tea and Sugar.*

OPPOSITE: *Loose tea scented with petals and rose-heads, served with Rose-scented Sugar and Rose-water Biscuits would make an unusual afternoon tea for a special occasion.*

ℛOSE TEATIME

𝒥n summer, when garden roses are in glorious abundance, you can use the fragrant petals to make rose jelly to spread on scones with lashings of clotted cream. Less indulgent are delicious rose-petal sandwiches.

ℛOSE JELLY

This pretty pink jelly can be used to sweeten yogurts or fromage frais, as a condiment with cold roasted chicken and to flavour light meat sauces. This makes 500 g (1¼ lb).

INGREDIENTS
500 g/1¼ lb/2 cups sugar
750 ml/1¼ pints/3 cups water
300 g (11 oz) scented rose petals
175 ml/6 fl oz/¾ cup lemon juice
75 ml (5 tbsp) commercial pectin
75 ml (5 tbsp) rose-water

1 Dissolve the sugar in the water with the petals and lemon juice by heating gently in a large saucepan. Bring to the boil and simmer for about 30 minutes. Turn into a large nylon sieve lined with muslin or use a jelly bag set over a bowl. Leave to drip through overnight.

2 Add the pectin and rose-water to the liquid and bring to the boil until setting point is reached (104°C/ 220°F on a sugar thermometer). Remove from the heat and decant into warmed, sterilized jars. Cover with cellophane circles and seal.

ℛOSE-PETAL SANDWICHES

These dainty sandwiches make a healthier alternative to cake or biscuits and may be served with a refreshing cup of rose-scented tea or a rose-hip tisane.

INGREDIENTS
225 g/8 oz/1 cup unsalted butter
5 heads scented dark pink or red
*   roses*
1 loaf soft bread, very thinly sliced

1 Cut the block of butter in half lengthways and place each half on a dish lined with a thick layer of rose petals. Cover the sides and top of the butter generously with more petals. Cover with a lid or layer of muslin and leave for 24 hours in the larder section of the refrigerator.

2 Discard the top layer of petals and allow the butter to soften slightly before spreading on to slices of bread. Use a heart-shaped pastry cutter to cut out the centre of each slice and add a thin layer of fresh rose petals before putting the slices together to make sandwiches.

RIGHT: *A complete rose tea, decorated with 'Black Tea', 'Shocking Blue' and pale pink miniature roses.*

ROSE WINES AND PUNCHES

There is a freshness and intensity of flavour in home-made wines and punches that is very rarely present in commercial counterparts.

It is also fun making your own drinks to serve to guests on a hot summer's day. The extra effort you have put into your al fresco party will not go

unnoticed. These recipes are meant to be drunk the same day – if making them in advance, keep them cool in the refrigerator.

ABOVE: *The pendulous hips in the centre are* Rosa moyesii, *which has pinky-red single flowers; the black hips are* Rosa pimpinellifolia, *a very ancient Scottish rose, bearing masses of creamy-white flowers; the hips in the trug on the left are 'Frau Dagmar Hartopp', a rose pink, single-bloom flower which grows on a very fresh green compact bush bearing crimson hips; the hips on the right are 'Hansa', large and full with a red-violet colour; the hips in the bucket are 'Scabrosa', another rugosa hybrid, with velvet crimson-mauve single blooms and fat, rich hips.*

ℛOSE-HIP WINE

Traditionally, hedgerow rose-hips were gathered to make wine but if you do not live in the country, you could grow a hedge of *Rosa rugosa*, a vigorous species that produces exceptionally large, round hips. This rose makes enough wine to fill approximately six bottles.

INGREDIENTS
1 kg/2¼ lb/9 cups rose-hips
4.5 litres (8 pints) boiling water
1 kg/2¼ lb/3½ cups granulated sugar
juice of 1 lemon and 1 orange
15 g (½ oz) fresh baker's yeast

Mince the rose-hips roughly in a food processor, put into a plastic bucket and pour the boiling water over them. Stir with a long-handled wooden spoon. Leave to stand for 3 days, stirring daily. Strain the juice through a jelly bag.

Make a syrup by heating the sugar with the fruit juices. Add the syrup to the rose-hip juice and pour into a fermentation jar. Cream the yeast with a little of the liquid, leave to ferment, then add to the wine. Add more boiled, cooled water to bring the liquid to within 2.5 cm (1 in) of the top of the jar. Fit an airlock and leave in a warm place to ferment. Rack into a clean jar, leave for a further 3 months and then bottle.

ℛOSE-PETAL PUNCH

Fragrant rose petals can be used both to flavour and decorate modest sparkling wines to create a celebratory punch, perfect for a party on a summer's day. This serves about eight people.

INGREDIENTS
300 g (11 oz) scented rose petals
90 g/3½ oz/⅓ cup caster sugar
105 ml (7 tbsp) framboise (raspberry liqueur)
1 bottle dry white wine, chilled
1 bottle demi-sec sparkling wine or champagne, chilled
extra petals or blooms, to decorate

BELOW: *The roses used to decorate and flavour this punch are the shrub 'Felicia'.*

1 Sprinkle the petals with sugar, pour over the framboise, cover and chill. Add the wine and chill once more.

2 Pour through a sieve into a jug. Add the sparkling wine or champagne. Decorate with rose petals.

ROSE CORDIAL, JAM AND VINEGAR

To make the most of the wonderful array of rose petals in the summer months, here are some inspirational recipes for a delicious cordial, a tasty jam and an unusual salad vinegar, all designed to enhance your guests' table.

ROSE-PETAL CORDIAL

A light refreshing drink to serve at any time of day in early summer when roses are in abundance.

INGREDIENTS
25 heads scented roses
900 g/2 lb/4 cups granulated sugar
2 litres/3½ pints/8 cups boiled or
    bottled still water, chilled
½ lemon, preferably unwaxed, sliced
sparkling mineral water
extra petals, to decorate

1 Remove the rose petals carefully from the heads and put into a large pan or bowl, with the sugar, water and sliced lemon. Stir three or four times during a 24-hour period.

2 Strain and decant into clean glass bottles. Dilute to taste with the mineral water, adding fresh rose petals for decoration.

ROSE-PETAL JAM

A delicate preserve for scones with cream. It makes 675 g (1½ lb).

INGREDIENTS
600 g/3 lb/6 cups granulated sugar
750 ml/1¼pints/3 cups water
150 g (5 oz) scented rose petals
175 ml/6 fl oz/¾ cup lemon juice
75 ml (5 tbsp) commercial pectin
45 ml (3 tbsp) rose-water

1 Dissolve the sugar in the water with the petals and lemon juice by heating gently in a large saucepan. Bring to the boil and simmer for about 30 minutes.

2 Add the pectin and rose-water and stir together. Boil hard for 5 minutes. Test for setting point (104°C/220°F), using a sugar thermometer. Alternatively, put a teaspoonful of jam on a cold saucer and put in the refrigerator for about 5 minutes. Then tilt the saucer and if the jam does not run, it is ready for potting. It is wise to test every few minutes to avoid over-boiling.

3 Leave the jam to cool for 10 minutes and then pour carefully into warmed, sterilized jars. Cover with cellophane circles and seal. When the jars are completely cold, label and date the jam.

RIGHT: Rose-flavoured cordial, jam and vinegar capture the essence of summer.

ℛOSE-PETAL VINEGAR

This delicately scented vinegar can be used in a dressing for summer salads and, sparingly, in fruit salads. It is also effective as a cool compress, to ease a nagging headache.

INGREDIENTS
300 ml/1½ pint/1¼ cups good quality
  white wine vinegar
scented red rose petals

1 Pull the rose petals from the flower-heads. Scald the vinegar by bringing it to just below boiling point and allow to cool.

2 Snip off the bitter white part at the base of each petal. Prepare enough petals to fill a cup and put into a large glass jar or bottle.

ABOVE: Rose-petal Vinegar is delicious on salads, either in a dressing or on its own.

3 *(Left)* Add the cooled vinegar, seal very tightly with a screw-top or cork and leave on a sunny window sill for at least 3 weeks.

ROSE HONEY AND SHORTBREAD

Rose-water is a delightful and adaptable ingredient; added to cakes and biscuits, it gives them that subtle taste of summer.

ROSE-PETAL HONEY

This aromatic honey makes an inexpensive and thoughtful gift and is reputed to relieve sore throats and raspy coughs. This recipe will make 115 g/4 oz/⅓ cup.

INGREDIENTS
115 g/4 oz/ ⅓ cup pale, runny,
    preferably organic, honey
25 g/1 oz/5 cups scented rose petals

1 Put the honey and rose petals in an enamel pan and boil gently for 10 minutes. Strain the honey while it is still quite hot and put into a warmed, sterilized jar with a tight-fitting lid. When the jar is cold, label and date the honey.

ABOVE: *The rose here is 'Amber Queen', but any scented rose petals can be added to the honey.*

ROSE-WATER BISCUITS

Light, crunchy biscuits that are easy to make and bake in minutes.

INGREDIENTS
225 g/8 oz/1 cup slightly salted
    butter
225 g/8 oz/1 cup caster sugar
1 size 1–2 egg
15 ml (1 tbsp) single cream
275 g/10 oz/2½ cups plain flour
2.5 ml (½ tsp) salt
5 ml (1 tsp) baking powder
15 ml (1 tbsp) rose-water
caster sugar for sprinkling

1 Preheat the oven to 190°C/375°F/ Gas Mark 5. Soften the butter and mix with all the other ingredients until you have a firm dough. Mould the mixture into an even roll and wrap in greaseproof paper. Chill until it is firm enough to slice very thinly. This may take 1–1½ hours.

2 Line baking sheets with non-stick baking parchment and arrange the biscuits on the sheets with enough space for them to spread. Sprinkle with a little caster sugar and bake for about 10 minutes until they are just turning brown at the edges.

FESTIVAL SHORTBREADS

This Greek version of shortbread keeps well for a long time in the delicately flavoured sugar, which may be used up in other recipes after the biscuits have been eaten.

INGREDIENTS

250 g/9 oz/1 generous cup unsalted or
    lightly salted butter
65 g/2½ oz/⅓ cup caster sugar
1 size 1–2 egg yolk
30 ml (2 tbsp) Greek ouzo or brandy
115 g (4 oz) unblanched almonds
65 g/2½ oz/½ cup cornflour
300 g/11 oz/2¼ cups plain flour
about 60 ml (4 tbsp) triple-distilled
    rose-water
500 g/1¼ lb/2¾ cups icing sugar

1 Preheat the oven to 170–180°C/ 325–350°F/Gas Mark 3–4. Cream the butter and add the sugar, egg yolk and alcohol. Grind the almonds, skins and all: they should be much coarser and browner than commercially ground almonds. Add to the butter mixture and then work in the corn-flour and enough plain flour to give a firm, soft mixture (you may need a little more flour). You can mix it in an electric mixer or food processor.

2 Divide into 24–28 equal portions. Make them into little rolls and then form them into crescents around a finger. Place on baking trays lined with non-stick baking parchment and bake for 15 minutes. Check the biscuits and lower the temperature if they seem to be colouring. Bake for a further 5–10 minutes in any case. Leave them to cool.

3 Pour the rose-water into a small bowl and tip the sifted icing sugar into a larger one. Dip a biscuit into the rose-water, sprinkle it with icing sugar and place in an airtight tin. Repeat until all the biscuits are coated. Pack the biscuits loosely or they will stick together. Sift the remaining icing sugar over the biscuits and keep them in the airtight tin.

BELOW: (From left to right) Rose-water Biscuits, Rose-petal Honey and Festival Shortbread. The roses in the picture are 'Henri Matisse' and 'Grey Dawn'.

ROSE CHOCOLATES AND CANDIES

For special occasions, such as birthdays and at Christmas, hand made chocolates and candies make a delightfully indulgent gift.
Use decorative boxes or tins to contain the treats.

SWEDISH ROSE CHOCOLATE BALLS

This is a very rich chocolate sweet which could be easily made by children if the rum were omitted.

INGREDIENTS
150 g (5 oz) good quality dessert chocolate
30 ml (2 tbsp) ground almonds
30 ml (2 tbsp) caster sugar
2 size 1–2 egg yolks
10 ml (2 tsp) strong coffee or coffee essence
15 ml (1 tbsp) dark rum
15 ml (1 tbsp) triple-distilled rose-water
40 g/1½ oz/¼ cup chocolate vermicelli

1 Grind the chocolate and add to all the other ingredients, except the rose-water and vermicelli. Make into tiny balls by rolling small teaspoonfuls between your fingers. Chill well. Dip into the rose-water and roll in the chocolate vermicelli.

ROSE-PETAL TRUFFLES

An indulgent treat that demands the finest quality chocolate with at least 60% cocoa solids. You can replace the rose-water with brandy if you prefer a less sweet flavour.

INGREDIENTS
500 g (1¼ lb) plain chocolate
300 ml/½ pint/1¼ cups double cream
15 ml (1 tbsp) triple-distilled rose-water
2 drops rose essential oil
250 g (9 oz) plain chocolate, for coating
crystallized rose petals

ABOVE: Keep these truffles in the refrigerator.

1 Melt the chocolate and cream together in a double-boiler until completely combined and soft in texture. Add the rose-water and essential oil. Pour the mixture into a baking tin lined with non-stick baking parchment. Leave to cool.

2 When the mixture is nearly firm, take teaspoonfuls of the chocolate and shape into balls in your hands. Chill the truffles thoroughly until they are quite hard.

3 Melt the chocolate for coating the truffles in the double-boiler. Skewer a truffle and dip it into the melted chocolate, making sure it is completely covered. Leave the finished truffles on a sheet of non-stick baking parchment to cool, placing a crystallized rose petal on each one before the chocolate sets.

LEFT: Tie the chocolate balls up in a circle of clear cellophane with tiny pieces of raffia.

Rose Turkish Delight

In the Middle East, these sweets are served with tiny cups of very strong coffee.

Ingredients
60 ml (4 tbsp) triple-distilled rose-water
30 ml (2 tbsp) powdered gelatine
450 g/1 lb/1¼ cups granulated sugar
150 ml/¼ pint/⅔ cup water
cochineal colouring
9 drops rose essential oil
25 g/1 oz/¼ cup roughly chopped blanched almonds
20 g/¼ oz/scant ¼ cup cornflour
65 g/2½ oz/⅓ cup icing sugar

1 Pour the rose-water into a bowl and sprinkle on the gelatine. Dissolve the granulated sugar in the water in a saucepan over a low heat. When the syrup is clear, boil until the mixture reaches 116°C/234°F on a sugar thermometer.

2 Remove from the heat and add the gelatine and rose-water. Return to a low heat, stirring, until the gelatine has dissolved. Remove from the heat, and add a few drops of cochineal colouring. Add the rose oil and almonds and pour the syrupy mixture into a 15–18 cm (6–7 in) oiled baking tin and leave to set.

3 Cut into pieces. Sift the cornflour and icing sugar together and sprinkle on to the cut pieces.

RIGHT: Spear the Turkish delights with orange sticks to keep the sugar mixture from covering your hands.

$\mathcal{S}$PRAY OF ICING ROSES

ABOVE: *This spray of roses could be made in any colour to match your table setting.*

$\mathcal{I}$ncredibly realistic, this delicate spray of roses and rose-buds is easily made from the sugar paste sold for cake decorating, using a selection of clever tools. It makes a very definite statement as a cake decoration and would also be a lovely gift, presented in a beautiful box like a corsage.

MATERIALS
100 g (3½ oz) cyclamen sugar flower
    paste
covered florist's wire, cut into
    13 cm (5 in) lengths
small rolling pin
five-petal cutter
dog-bone tool
foam pad (optional)

fine paintbrush
100 g (3½ oz) green sugar flower
    paste
calyx cutter
set of rose-leaf cutters
cocktail stick
1 m (1 yd) narrow ribbon
florist's tape
scissors

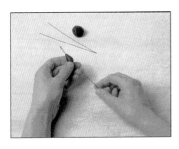

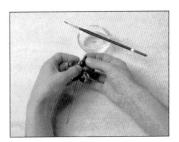

1 Roll a hazelnut-sized ball of cyclamen flower paste and mould it into a cone shape. Bend a small hook on the end of a length of wire and thread it through the top of the cone, until the loop is inside. Leave to dry completely.

2 Roll a small piece of cyclamen flower paste fairly thinly. Cut out rose petals with the cutter and thin the edges using a dog-bone tool, resting the petal on a foam pad or in the palm of your hand.

3 Insert the dry cone stem in the centre of the petals. Dampen each petal with water on a fine brush. Lift alternate petals to cling around the cone one at a time. Leave to dry. Then add further petals.

4 Roll out some green flower paste thinly. Cut a calyx with the cutter and thin the edges as before. Thread the wired rose through the centre and fix it with a little water. Roll a small cone of green flower paste and thread it on to the wire, to complete the rose and calyx. Make two buds and three larger roses altogether.

5 To make the leaves: roll out some green flower paste, leaving a ridge down the middle. Cut the leaf out with a leaf cutter and mark veins with a cocktail stick. Holding the leaf between your fingers and thumb, insert a length of wire into the ridge. Twist the leaf, to make it more realistic, and leave to dry.

6 Make four large leaves, eleven medium leaves and ten small leaves. Make graduated sprays of three or five leaves and tape them together, using thin strips of florist's tape.

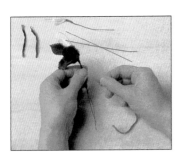

7 (Left) Wrap a length of ribbon around to make two loops of different sizes. Trim the ends and tape on to a length of wire. Cut the larger loop into two uneven lengths. Make several more ribbon loops in the same way. Arrange a leaf spray, ribbon loop and rose together and tape the stems.

8 Arrange the sprays into a larger bouquet, and tape the stems. Fold the wire ends and tape.

CELEBRATION ROSE AND FRUIT CAKE

This deliciously rich fruit cake is perfect for celebrations such as birthdays or christenings. Covered with a delicately flavoured rose-water icing, it is decorated with whole edible crystallized rose blooms. It makes a 20 cm (8 in) round or 18 cm (7 in) square cake.

INGREDIENTS

175 g/6 oz/1 cup sultanas
375 g/12 oz/2¼ cups currants
175 g/6 oz/1 cup raisins
15 ml (1 tbsp) brandy or very strong
    rose-hip tea
225 g/8 oz/2 cups plain flour
7.5 ml (1½ tsp) ground mixed spice
2.5 ml (½ tsp) ground nutmeg
2.5 ml (½ tsp) ground cinnamon
generous pinch of salt
105 g/3¼ oz/¾ cup butter or
    margarine
105 g/3¼ oz/¾ cup soft brown sugar
2.5 ml (½ tsp) grated orange rind
3 size 2 eggs
65 g/2½ oz/⅓ cup glacé cherries
40 g/1½ oz/¼ cup candied orange
    peel
40 g/1½ oz/¼ cup chopped almonds
15 ml (1 tbsp) black treacle
rose jelly
icing sugar
crystallized rose blooms,
    to decorate

1 Preheat the oven to 140°C/275°F/ Gas Mark 1. Mix the dried fruits with the brandy or rose-hip tea in a large bowl, cover and leave to macerate overnight. Grease and line the base and sides of a 20 cm (8 in) round or 18 cm (7 in) square cake tin.

2 Sift the flour, spices and salt together in a large bowl. In a separate bowl, beat the butter or margarine, sugar and orange rind together until light and creamy. Add 15 ml (1 tbsp) of the flour mixture before adding each of the eggs to the butter mixture. Fold in the remaining flour mixture and stir in the macerated fruit, glacé cherries, candied peel, almonds and treacle.

3 Spoon the mixture into the prepared tin (pan) and level the surface. Cover the top with a double layer of non-stick baking parchment with a 2.5 cm (1 in) diameter air-hole cut in the centre. Tie a double layer of parchment around the outside of the tin (pan), so it stands at least 5 cm (2 in) above the rim. This is important as it prevents the cake from burning. Bake the cake on the lowest shelf for 4½ hours; do not open the door while it is cooking. Leave to cool before removing the tin and icing.

FONDANT ROSE ICING

INGREDIENTS

900 g/2 lb/5½ cups icing sugar
2 egg whites
5 ml (1 tsp) triple-distilled rose-water
2.5 ml (½ tsp) lemon juice
120 ml/4 fl oz/½ cup liquid glucose

1 Sieve the icing sugar into a bowl and beat in the egg whites, rose-water, lemon juice and liquid glucose with a wooden spoon. Knead until the mixture forms a firm dough.

2 Spread the cake top and sides with rose jelly. Roll out the icing on a surface dredged with icing sugar.

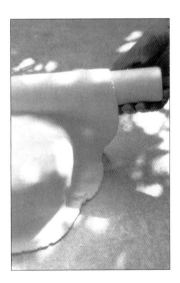

3 Rub the surface of the icing with icing sugar to give an even covering. Use the rolling pin to position the icing over the cake. Cut off any excess. Decorate with crystallized roses.

LEFT: *Gently remove the crystallized rose petals before eating.*

CRYSTALLIZED ROSE PETALS

*I*t is essential, of course, that the rose petals used for any of these recipes are collected from bushes that have not been sprayed with any sort of pesticide and are not growing near a busy road. Pick fresh full blooms carefully, rinse and dry the petals thoroughly, and then remove the white triangle at the base of each petal. When crystallizing complete blooms, leave a short piece of stem to hold them by.

MATERIALS
rose petals or flower-heads
egg white, lightly beaten
paintbrush
icing sugar, sifted
wire rack
tissue paper

ABOVE: *Crystallized rose-heads and petals are a delicious way to decorate cakes and desserts.*

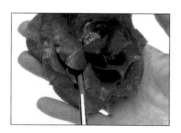

1 Each petal or bloom must be completely covered with a thin, even layer of lightly beaten egg white. Use a paintbrush that gets right into the cracks and crevices and do not forget the undersides of the petals. Any uncoated parts will turn brown and shrivel up. The process must be done quickly before the egg white dries. After the third or fourth rose you will get the knack.

2 Sprinkle sifted icing sugar over evenly and shake off the excess, otherwise any blobs will cause a patchy effect. This may be desirable to create light and shade contrast but a regular and even coating will preserve the roses more successfully.

3 Allow petals or blooms to dry on a wire rack. Stored between layers of tissue paper, the petals will keep for about a week. Do not put crystallized petals or flowers in the refrigerator or they will "weep" – keep in a dry and cool place.

ROSE AND RASPBERRY CHEESECAKE

As well as having rose flavours in your desserts, it is also a lovely idea to decorate your dishes with crystallized rose petals. They add a winning touch to any display.

INGREDIENTS
200 g (7 oz) shortcrust pastry
egg yolk, for brushing pastry
175 g/6 oz/¾ cup quark or skimmed
    milk soft cheese
5 ml (1 tsp) finely grated, preferably
    unwaxed, lemon rind
45 ml (3 tbsp) strained Greek yoghurt
10 ml (2 tsp) triple-distilled rose-
    water
15 ml (1 tbsp) caster sugar
350 g/12 oz/3 cups raspberries
    (or combination of soft fruits)
30 ml (2 tbsp) Rose Jelly
    (or redcurrant jelly)
crystallized rose petals or blooms,
    to decorate

BELOW: This light summer tart could be made with a combination of fruits, such as strawberries and red and white currants.

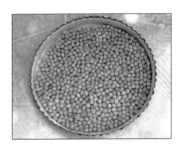

1 Preheat the oven to 200°C/400°F/ Gas Mark 6. Line a well buttered, fluted 20 cm (8 in) flan tin with the pastry and prick with a fork. Cover the pastry base with baking parchment and fill with baking beans or dried chick-peas. Brush the edges with egg yolk and bake for 15 minutes. Remove the paper and beans and cook for a further 10 minutes, or until the pastry is golden. Cool in the tin.

2 Cream the soft cheese and blend with the lemon rind, yogurt, rose-water and sugar. Fill the cooled pastry case and spread smoothly. Arrange the raspberries around the edge of the cheesecake. Heat the jelly until runny and brush over the raspberries. For special occasions, decorate with crystallized rose petals or whole blooms.

ℛose PASHKA

ABOVE: *The delicate rose decorations add elegance and interest to this dish.*

*ℐ*n Russia, a version of this creamy dessert is traditionally served at Easter, made in a special wooden mould; a simple clay flower pot, washed and scrubbed well and baked in a hot oven for 30 minutes, will do just as well.

INGREDIENTS
60 ml (4 tbsp) single cream
2 size 1–2 egg yolks
75 g/3 oz/¹/₃ cup caster sugar
90 g/3¹/₂ oz/scant ¹/₂ cup unsalted butter, softened
350 g/12 oz/1¹/₂ cups curd cheese
350 g/12 oz/1¹/₂ cups mascarpone cheese
10 ml (2 tsp) triple-distilled rose-water
50 g/2 oz/¹/₂ cup chopped candied peel
50 g/2 oz/¹/₂ cup chopped blanched almonds
crystallized rose blooms, to decorate

1 Heat the cream to just below boiling point. Beat the egg yolks with the sugar until light and foamy and add to the cream. Heat together in a saucepan until the mixture thickens, taking care not to let it boil and curdle. Remove from the heat and cool. Beat the butter until creamy and add to the egg and cream mixture, adding the cheeses slowly then the rose-water, candied peel and nuts. Line the terracotta pot with muslin and spoon the mixture into it, covering the top with muslin.

2 Weight a small plate on the top of the flower pot and stand it on a plate in the refrigerator for about 6 hours or overnight. Turn out the pashka by inverting the flower pot on to a serving dish and remove the muslin. Decorate the edge of the dish with the crystallized roses.

ROSE-PETAL PAVLOVA

If you are making ice cream, a delicious way to use up the egg white is to make a pavlova.

INGREDIENTS
4 size 1–2 egg whites
175 g/6 oz/ ¾ cup caster sugar
60 ml (4 tbsp) Rose Jelly
  (or redcurrant jelly)
300 ml/ ½ pint/1¼ cups double cream,
  whipped, or fromage frais
300 g/11 oz/2¾ cups mixed soft fruits
fresh and crystallized rose petals,
  to decorate

1 Preheat the oven to 140°C/275°F/ Gas Mark 1. Cut a baking parchment circle and place on a baking tray. Whisk the egg whites until stiff and slowly whisk in the sugar, until the mixture makes stiff, glossy peaks. Spoon the meringue on to the paper circle, making a slight indentation in the centre and soft crests around the outside. Bake for 1–1½ hours, until the meringue is crisp. Take care not to let it turn brown. Leave the meringue to cool in the oven.

2 Immediately before serving, melt the jelly over a low heat and spread it in the centre. Spoon over the whipped cream or fromage frais and arrange the soft fruits and rose petals on top. The dish should be eaten straight away.

BELOW: Why not make the Pavlova the table centrepiece, by surrounding it with fresh greenery from the garden?

$\mathcal{S}$OURCES AND SUPPLIERS

UK

ROSE SOCIETIES

The Royal National Rose Society
(membership includes free publications, advice, shows
and garden visits)
contact The Secretary
The Royal National Rose Society
Chiswell Green
St Albans
Herts AL2 3NR
Tel: 01727 850461

British Rose Growers
  Association
303 Mile End Road
Colchester
Essex
CO4 5EA

ROSE GROWERS
(including Old Roses, personal shoppers and by mail
  order)

David Austin Roses
Bowling Green Lane
Albrighton
Wolverhampton WV7 3HB
Tel: 01902 373931

Le Grice Roses
Norwich Road
North Walsham
Norfolk NR28 0DR
Tel: 01692 402591

Peter Beales Roses
London Road
Attleborough
Norfolk NR17 1AY
Tel: 01953 454707

Cottage Garden Roses
Woodlands House
Stretton
near Stafford ST19 9LG
Tel: 01785 840217

ESSENTIAL OIL SUPPLIERS
(shops and mail order)

Neal's Yard Remedies
5 Golden Cross
Cornmarket Street
Oxford OX1 3EU
Tel: 01865 245436

Culpeper Ltd
Hadstock Road
Linton
Cambridge
CB1 6NJ
Tel: 01440 788196

DRIED ROSES
(personal shoppers and mail order)

The Hop Shop
Castle Farm
Shoreham
Sevenoaks
Kent TN14 7UB
Tel: 01959 523219

US

ROSE SOCIETIES

American Rose Society
Box 300000
Shreveport, LA 711390
Tel: (318) 938 5402

Heritage Roses Foundation
Mr. Charles A. Walker Jr.
1512 Gorman St
Raleigh, NC 27606

American Horticultural Society
7931 East Boulevard Drive
Alexandria, VA 22308
Tel: (703) 768 5700

ROSE GROWERS (including mail order suppliers)

Armstrong Roses
P O Box 4220
Huntington Station, NY 11746
Tel: (800) 321 6640

Lowe's Own-root Roses
6 Sheffield Road
Nashua, NH 03062
Tel: (603) 888 2214

Jackson and Perkins
1 Rose Lane
Medford, OR 97501
Tel: (800) USA-ROSE

NATURAL BEAUTY INGREDIENTS

The Body Shop
45 Horse Hill Road
Cedar Knolls, NY 07927 2014
Tel: (800) 541 2535

Kiehl's
109 Third Avenue
New York, NY 10002
Tel: (212) 677 3171

Lorann Oils
P O Box 22009
Lansing, MI 48909-2009
Tel: (800) 248 1302

SUPPLIERS OF DRIED FLOWERS (shops and mail order)

Dody Lyness Co.
7336 Berry Hill Drive
Polos Verdes Peninsula, CA 90274
Tel: (310) 377 7040

Gailann's Floral Catalog
821 W. Atlantic Street
Branson, MO 65616

Nature's Finest
P O Box 10311, Dept. CSS
Burke, VA 22009

AUSTRALIA

ROSE SOCIETIES

National Rose Society
271B Belmore Road
North Balwyn, Vic 3104
Tel: (03) 9857 9656

Rose Society in Victoria
P. O. Box 1004
Blackburn North Vic 3130
Tel: (03) 9877 4301

Rose Society of NSW
299 Malton Road
North Epping NSW 2121
Tel: (02) 869 7516

Queensland Rose Society Inc
GPO Box 1866
Brisbane Qld 4001
Tel: (07) 814 4714

Rose Society of South Australia
29 Columbia Crescent
Modbury North SA 5092
Tel: (002) 663 366

Rose Society of Tasmania
RSD 146 Cradoc Hill Road
Cradoc Hill Tas 7109
Tel: (002) 458 6452

Rose Society of W.A.
33 Lord St
Bentley WA 6102
Tel: (09) 458 6452

ROSE GROWERS AND NURSERIES

The Perfumed Garden
895 Derril Road
Moorooduc
Victoria 3933

Swane's Nursery
490 Galston Road
Dural
NSW, 2158
Tel: (02) 651 1322

Doyles Rose Farm
1389 Waterford Tambourine Road
Logan Village
QLD 4207
Tel: (07) 5546 8216

Brundrett & Sons (Roses) Pty Ltd
Brundrett Road
Narre Warren North
Victoria, 3804
Tel: (03) 9596 8742

SUPPLIERS

Hedgerow Flowers
177 King William Road
Hyde Park
SA 5061
Tel: (08) 373 4779

Roses Only
Shop 12, Chifley Plaza
Chifley Square
Sydney NSW 2000
Tel: (02) 232 4499

The Gardener's Book
  Service
211 Bay Street
Brighton
Victoria 3186
Tel: (03) 9596 8742

INDEX

Notes

NOTES

NOTES

NOTES

NOTES

NOTES

NOTES

NOTES